GET YOUR SHIP TOGETHER

GET YOUR SHIP
TOGETHER

HOW GREAT LEADERS INSPIRE OWNERSHIP
FROM THE KEEL UP

D. Michael Abrashoff

PORTFOLIO

PORTFOLIO
Published by the Penguin Group
Penguin Group (USA) Inc., 375 Hudson Street,
New York, New York 10014, U.S.A.
Penguin Group (Canada), 10 Alcorn Avenue,
Toronto, Ontario, Canada M4V 3B2
(a division of Pearson Penguin Canada Inc.)
Penguin Books Ltd, 80 Strand, London WC2R 0RL, England
Penguin Ireland, 25 St. Stephen's Green, Dublin 2, Ireland
(a division of Penguin Books Ltd)
Penguin Books Australia Ltd, 250 Camberwell Road, Camberwell,
Victoria 3124, Australia
(a division of Pearson Australia Group Pty Ltd)
Penguin Books India Pvt Ltd, 11 Community Centre, Panchsheel Park,
New Delhi – 110 17, India
Penguin Group (NZ), Cnr Airborne and Rosedale Roads, Albany,
Auckland 1310, New Zealand
(a division of Pearson New Zealand Ltd)
Penguin Books (South Africa) (Pty) Ltd, 24 Sturdee Avenue,
Rosebank, Johannesburg 2196, South Africa

Penguin Books Ltd, Registered Offices:
80 Strand, London WC2R 0RL, England

First published in 2005 by Portfolio,
a member of Penguin Group (USA) Inc.

10   9   8   7   6   5   4   3   2   1

Copyright © D. Michael Abrashoff, 2004
All rights reserved

CIP data available

ISBN 1-59184-074-0

This book is printed on acid-free paper. ∞

Printed in the United States of America
Set in Adobe Garamond
Designed by Daniel Lagin

JAN 1 9 2005

This book is dedicated to the wonderful men and women in uniform today, both civilian and military, who are keeping us safe.

ACKNOWLEDGMENTS

I AM ONE OF THE LUCKIEST PEOPLE ON THIS PLANET WHO HAD Mary and Don (who passed away in May 2003) Abrashoff as parents. We never had much money in our family, but I can't think of one thing we lacked growing up. I once asked Dad, "What was the best investment you ever made?" His answer: "Making sure my seven children got educated." I have no idea what the future holds economically for this country, but if we are to maintain our competitive edge, it will begin and end with education. My mother, now eighty-two, still substitute teaches one or two days a week in the Altoona (Pennsylvania) School District and in the area vocational-technical school. She's my role model for helping to keep our great country strong.

I would like to thank the talented writers, editors, and researchers at Word-works—Donna Carpenter, Maurice Coyle, Ruth Hlavacek, Larry Martz, Barbara Nelson, Toni Porcelli, Cindy Sammons, Robert Shnayerson, Robert Stock, and Ellen Wojahn. They have made our team great. I hope to be able to continue to write books with them for many years to come. They are the best.

I also want to thank Helen Rees, my own Jerry Maguire and the best damn literary agent in the world! She has also become one of my dearest friends. I can't think of a better way to start the day than a 5:30 A.M. phone conversation with Helen, discussing world events.

Thanks also to Harry Rhodes, Tony D'Amelio, and the rest of the gang at the Washington Speakers Bureau. They do a wonderful job for me and their clients. They are truly a class act. Special recognition must go to Karen McMahon and Joy Nagle, who drew the short straws and got stuck planning my travel arrangements and enduring my assorted stories about the indignities of air travel today.

And most of all, I continue to be grateful to the U.S. Navy for all the opportunities I was given, and for my wonderful crew on USS *Benfold*.

CONTENTS

ACKNOWLEDGMENTS   vii

INTRODUCTION   xi

CHAPTER 1
First Lieutenant Buddy Gengler Calls for Help
and Saves His Troops   1

CHAPTER 2
CEO Trish Karter Makes the Deer Dance   39

CHAPTER 3
CEO Roger Valine Demands a Great Deal from
Everyone—and Gives a Great Deal Back   68

CHAPTER 4
Captain Al Collins Follows to Lead   92

CHAPTER 5
VP Laura Folse Is an Alchemist at BP   131

CHAPTER 6
Officer-in-Charge Ward Clapham Transforms
the Mounties   156

EPILOGUE   196

INDEX   199

INTRODUCTION

MY NEW LIFE AS THE CAPTAIN OF USS *BENFOLD* BEGAN ON A gleaming day in San Diego Bay. A high sun warmed the salt air to a perfect 73 degrees; the pale blue horizon, flecked with white sails, blended seamlessly into an indigo sea. And there I was on the bridge of a billion-dollar navy warship, a thirty-six-year-old master of the universe lounging casually in the captain's chair, as I prepared to take my ship out to sea for the first time.

Benfold was a beautiful fighting machine—a destroyer armed with the navy's most advanced guided missiles, a radar system that could home in on a bird-sized object fifty miles away, and a presumably superb crew of 310 men and women. With four gas turbine engines at my fingertips, I could push this 8,300-ton leviathan to more than thirty knots—at least thirty-three miles an hour—sending up a massive rooster tail in her wake.

My adrenaline was flowing. The moment I had been waiting for my entire career was at hand. The tugboats were alongside, standing by for the order to guide us away from the pier.

Despite all that power and sophisticated machinery, and no matter how good a ship handler the captain may be, we still need tugboats to help steer us into and out of our berth. Mooring to and getting under way from the pier are two of our most difficult maneuvers. Lots of things can go wrong—you can smash into the wharf or into ships behind you, or run the ship aground. If any of those things were to happen, I could get fired almost on the spot; my head would roll even before the investigation started.

Also, right underneath the bow of the ship is a huge, bulbous sonar dome covered by a black rubber protective device. Think of it as a five-million-dollar steel-belted radial tire. If it scrapes the curb (read *pier*), you can decrease the sonar's ability to detect submarines. Or, worst case, you can puncture the protective shield and deflate it completely. So prudence dictates that we use tugs to move us away from the pier.

Now, with the engines just whispering at idle speed, their vast stores of power bridled, we prepared to shove off. What a kick. I was bursting with pride. I couldn't wait to hit the open sea and order all engines ahead, flank speed.

I gave the order to take in all lines, directed the tugs to start backing us slowly from the pier, and then, like air whooshing out of a balloon, my ego cruise ended before it ever got under way. *Benfold* suddenly lost power. Her engines quit turning. In an instant, she became nothing but 8,300 tons of steel likely to run aground or crash into another ship. In the eerie silence, red warning lights blinked everywhere. I dashed into the pilothouse, fumbling for emergency phones, demanding information. At that moment, I was enormously relieved and grateful to have the tugboats hovering nearby like watchful parents running alongside a kid on a new bike. I ordered the tugs to push us back to the pier while we investigated the power failure.

When a ship loses power abruptly, you have four chances to avoid disaster. You can kick-start the engines by shooting a jet of high-pressure air into the turbines. Like an old-fashioned hand crank, the air jolt gets everything spinning and firing up again. If the first attempt fails, you have three flasks of emergency air for three more tries. But if those don't work, that's it—your ship is dead in the water, a useless and dangerous hulk that has to be towed back to port. That is the ultimate disgrace, rare but not unheard of.

Benfold lost power and unmade my day because at least one of the watch standers had not followed procedure. Whenever a ship is under way, the watch standers constantly monitor dials and gauges on the bridge and in the engine room to make sure all the parts of the huge, complex vessel are in sync. If anything goes wrong, they have to react in time to prevent further damage and engine failure. When *Benfold*'s watch standers failed to respond in time, a cascading series of events was set in train—much like the massive power outage on the East Coast in the summer of 2003—and the engines shut down to prevent serious damage. With the ship about to cast off the tugs in the narrow channel, disaster had been only seconds away.

We were lucky. Members of the engineering crew came to the rescue and got the engines up and running again in about fifty seconds. My mind was racing just as fast: I had been taught that a captain must be always alert, prepared for any disaster that could materialize in a given situation. Before backing away from the pier, I should have envisioned every possible scenario and had a preplanned response to deal with it. Whether from youthful inexperience or plain old cockiness, I didn't. We were just lucky the tugboats were still there to save us from disaster. Luck, though, is not a sound strategy for success.

With time I would come to understand that being the captain when times are good is easy. But true leaders must also prepare for what might happen when times are tough. Sometimes you have to steer a big ship near shoal water and that takes extra skill. The captain's biggest challenge is to be able to navigate wisely under any circumstances, expected or not.

Why was I so unready for a thoroughly possible crisis? How should I train myself and my crew for the inevitable next time?

I would soon learn that I could order a mission to be accomplished, but I couldn't order great results. Real leaders lay the cornerstone around which a team comes together to produce superior results. A mission based on luck or hope is not sustainable over the long haul.

Had I been directing *Benfold*'s castoff and departure like a winning leader, I would have behaved very differently. Real leadership is caring so intensely about something under your control—a ship, say—that you prepare for its success in both good times and bad. As *Benfold*'s fledgling captain, I quickly learned the importance of making sure that every sailor on the ship understood that he or she had a stake in guaranteeing *Benfold*'s readiness for war, peace, or anything in between.

As you may have read in my first book, *It's Your Ship,* I soon learned how tough—and rewarding—it is to turn 310 sailors into teammates who really care about the mission. Not me-firsters, but true collaborators. Winners in any weather. Since leaving the navy almost four years ago, I've learned that the same thing can be accomplished in civilian life if you understand the components needed to ensure success.

First and foremost, you must have a sound business strategy that values technical competence. You may even be able to get by on technical competency alone. But truly great results will only come when all crew members believe not only that what they are doing is important, but also understand that delivering great results every day serves their own best interests. With the right strategy and first-rate leadership, nearly any human enterprise can become a winner. That's why I wrote this book: to share real stories of unsung leadership derived not only from the U.S. military, but from all kinds of fields and organizations, private and public alike.

My own reeducation as a leader began out of disgust at myself, a sharp reaction to my unreadiness when *Benfold* lost power that beautiful San Diego morning. From then on, I trained and retrained myself for emergencies, those sudden jolts when there is no time to think and you have to switch to autopilot. To make that shift successfully requires a repertoire of reflexes. Forward planning is essential. To minimize damage, you have to anticipate and rehearse the first few steps to be taken in a crisis. I hadn't done that. Furthermore, I had forgotten that remedial action should begin with the captain—me.

For my entire tour as captain, I constantly tried to visualize worst-case scenarios and what I would do in response. Was I compulsive? Absolutely! But it wasn't because I wanted that next promotion. I could live without getting promoted, but I couldn't live with myself if one of my crew members got seriously injured or killed on my watch because of my failure to be prepared. I know that every other military leader in uniform today feels the same way. I hope and pray that our civilian leaders in the Pentagon share that sentiment.

Always preparing for trouble, I became a walking database of contingency plans for everything from a man or woman overboard to World War III. Missiles, plagues, terrorists, heart attacks—I envisioned all those and more. One dawn, I even woke up in a cold sweat after dreaming that terrorists had stolen my dress white uniform, leaving me in my skivvies just as the president of the United States was piped aboard to inspect *Benfold*. I immediately went out and bought a second set of dress whites—just in case.

My sailors sometimes thought I was nuts. The captain's eyes were peeled for terrorists whenever *Benfold* pulled into a port in the Middle East, so we manned additional watch stations in port for protection. It was 1997, a year after a terrorist bomb had exploded outside the U.S. portion of the Khobar Towers housing complex in Saudi Arabia, killing nineteen servicemen and wounding hundreds of others, civilians and military personnel alike. Having stood in the four-hundred-foot crater left by the blast, and being ever mindful of the senseless loss of lives, I was determined that we would not be caught unprepared.

Even after receiving an e-mail from a commodore telling me to relax, I couldn't. There was no history of terrorist attacks on a navy ship in port, he reminded me, and no intelligence that would lead the navy to believe an attack was coming. Maybe so, but it wasn't his crew that I was worried about. The deadly attack on USS *Cole* came three years later.

All this ever ready research did pay off, especially when I asked my ablest sailors how they would handle the nasty situations I imagined. Example: Suppose we're towing a million-dollar array of sonar hydrophones on antisubmarine patrol, and the umbilical line runs too shallow and wraps itself around our propellers. What should we do? The answer: Nothing—it's too late. You must prevent it at all costs. Which means that if you lose power while the array is deployed, you have to race to the stern of the ship and manually reel in the cable, which can be up to a mile long, before it has a chance to wrap around the propellers.

Sometimes the crew had answers I hadn't thought of. Sometimes they came up blank. But I made sure that everyone was planning ahead and training to make the best of the worst. The more they got involved, of course, the greater their stake in the outcome. I could see it happening when certain bellwether sailors lost their uncomfortable smiles and instead began offering insightful comments on the challenge at hand. We weren't buddies and never could be. I was their captain. But my crew began to coalesce into a real team, working together on something beyond themselves.

That was a relief. A navy captain can't induce performance by handing out huge bonuses and stock options. The rewards and incentives at my disposal were mainly intangible—more responsibility, public praise, extra liberty, a medal, respect. Nevertheless, these are highly coveted in the closed world of shipboard culture. A captain who keeps rewarding sailors for excellence, instead of punishing them for mediocrity, can gradually tilt the entire crew in the right direction. That's why I was constantly on the lookout for sailors doing something right that I could reward.

Not that it was easy. I couldn't just order my sailors to become paragons. I was dealing with 310 individuals, and they had their share of screwups. I had to do lots of subtle coaxing, stroking, and plain old politicking.

Take one of my chief problems—*Benfold*'s engineering department. With a few bright exceptions, my engineers were far less skilled than I had assumed they would be when I took over. Before my arrival, the ship had actually flunked its engineering certification, which was virtually unheard of for a top-drawer fighting ship that was practically new. What's more, *Benfold* had barely passed the re-certification test. Had the ship failed again, an already venomous atmosphere would have become even more so.

My ship's weakest link was its engineering department. And to make matters worse, I had never served in the engineering department and did not have much technical expertise to offer. The chief engineer's job is the toughest on the ship. In the best of circumstances, serving in this position aboard a warship is so mentally and physically draining that a rotation normally lasts only eighteen months, at which point the typical chief engineer limps off the ship, shoulders stooped and brain practically fried. But our poor, tormented engineer served on *Benfold* at a time when the navy was grappling with a severe shortage of engineering officers, causing his tour of duty to be extended to three years. When I first met the man, I saw a chain-smoker with trembling hands and weary eyes. I wasn't entirely sure he would live through the night.

The engineer's main problem, it turned out, was that everyone had long blamed him—unfairly, as I came to realize—for whatever went wrong, notably the inspections that *Benfold* failed with monotonous regularity. All too often we rush to affix blame instead of fixing the problem. I wanted to fix the problem. Even a cursory examination showed me that the worst trouble lay within a few key positions beneath the chief engineer, staffed by people who lacked the technical skills needed to do their jobs. But he was too fine a leader to pass the blame. He took it squarely on his own shoulders.

Imagine all this rancor multiplied by a factor of ten, which was the state of things when recertification loomed. Because the engineers were busy getting the equipment up to speed, they had no time for cleaning the bilge, a filthy job done in the exceedingly cramped bowels of the ship. But no one gives extra points for difficult maneuvering in a limited space. The bilge must be clean to pass inspection, and that's that. With the engineers otherwise engaged, it fell to the rest of the crew to stop working on their own jobs and lend a hand. They spent several weeks, hating every minute of it. As you might imagine, everyone wound up blaming the chief engineer not only for the first certification failure, but for the agony of preparing for the retest.

Benfold did pass its engineering certification the second time because of heroic work by a few indomitable souls. But the outcome was such a squeaker that the ship's engineering reputation sank even further. By the time I came aboard, the engineers had lost any embryonic pride they might have gleaned from their ordeal. They put down their oars, saying in effect, "Whew, we don't have to do that again for another two years." More to the point, and much to their own detriment, they promptly jettisoned whatever knowledge and ambition they had acquired to pass the test.

Unfortunately, that isn't unusual. Many ships tend to give the regulations short shrift until an inspection comes due; then crew members cram 24/7 to get up to speed. In my view, you've got to make your crew see the larger picture: the inspection sets the bar for sailing the ship properly each and every day. Instead of peaks and valleys in performance, you need a steady state of excellence. Your goal is to be able to nail any inspection, any day, without prior notice.

And you should never have to depend on one extraordinary person to save the day. The price for such heroics is too high: not only will the standout's foot-dragging shipmates never know the joy of accomplishment, but the whole ship will be left at risk if the hero is injured or transferred. In other words, you need a crew that is totally clear about who owns the ship: they do. And when someone owns something as magnificent as *Benfold,* they not only guard, fix, paint, polish, and improve it. They also love it.

I clearly needed a reborn engineering team ASAP. I needed it rebuilt from the keel up, or at least from the bilge just over the keel. I wanted engineers obsessed with keeping this complex ship running like a well-tuned Ferrari in any weather, engineers who were respected by their shipmates. And I wanted our chief engineer to live happily ever after (which he has since he got his own ship to command).

Believe it or not, most of my dream actually came true. *Benfold* eventually became an award-winning ship, a model of combat readiness that raised the bar for the entire Pacific Fleet. A once dysfunctional vessel operated by a sullen, resentful group of sailors developed into a cohesive, smoothly functioning machine with a crew of inspired problem solvers who were gunning to beat every metric in the Pacific Fleet—and usually did. In fact, our extraordinary skill and competence with Tomahawk cruise missiles put us in a class by ourselves and made us the go-to ship in the simmering Middle East troubles of the late 1990s. But what was particularly heartening to me was our reenlistment success: contrary to the prevailing trend in the navy, *Benfold*'s sailors reupped at unheard-of rates. And why not? Having been made to understand that it was *their* ship, not mine, the crew realized the importance of their work and took great pride in their accomplishments. As a result, *Benfold* could rightfully lay claim to being the best damn ship in the navy.

How did it happen? You can get the full story from *It's Your Ship,* a best seller that chronicles my navy career. But in this very different book, I will describe leadership lessons gleaned from numerous fields that are applicable to businesses everywhere.

One of the key lessons I learned in the navy is that training—constant training—is crucial for top performance in any enterprise, whether you're a brain surgeon, a concert pianist, or a marine general. To that end, the navy has an excellent system for introducing practices that can make a ship successful. Known as the

PB for T (Planning Board for Training), it calls for a weekly meeting of the senior officers and chief petty officers representing every major program on the ship to plan the next week's activities and set priorities. On *Benfold,* my goal was to convert the PB for T from a perfunctory nuisance to a genuine performance enabler.

If real leadership is largely about spotting and defusing trouble, the navy's PB for T is the perfect exercise. The idea behind it is to anticipate problems before they explode. It's also a powerful antidote to the oft-heard complaint that leaders spend too much time responding to crises they could avoid if only they had the luxury of peering and planning ahead.

PB for T can be as elaborate or as elementary as the captain cares to make it. In my view, *Benfold* succeeded largely because our program was inclusive and interactive. Chaired by my second in command, the executive officer, the board included all five department heads and representatives of every program, from damage control to drug abuse, that cut across the entire ship. The planning was comprehensive. The engineers, for instance, knew when they had to be ready with extra power because a combat-systems exercise had been scheduled, while the chief corpsman knew when a slack period would allow crew members to schedule medical and dental appointments. People began making short-term plans only in the context of long-range and middle-range goals. The more they got involved, the less we got bogged down by sudden surprises.

But that didn't happen right away. In the first month or so after the power loss, the weekly PB for T often ended up in a squabble because people had their own agendas and couldn't agree on priorities for the ship as a whole. Subordinating individual interests to the common good was hard work. For me, it was a little like settling a new country.

It was tough overcoming old biases about the engineering department. An Aegis-class destroyer like *Benfold* is sleek and sexy with an array of neat toys, while the engineers, who toil in time-honored fashion, were viewed as a drag on performance. Traditionally, engineering training always came second or third behind training for activities like firing a torpedo or a Tomahawk missile. Ships tend to schedule more glamorous operations during the daylight hours, and the chief engineer gets his training time from midnight to 0600. That means his people work all day supporting the other departments' exercises, and then work all night too. Meanwhile, the captain and the executive officer are fast asleep, oblivious to the opportunity to help the engineers improve their training.

A more discouraging, negative atmosphere is hard to imagine. You can't treat engineers like no-accounts and then expect them to perform flawlessly. If you treat people poorly, they will perform poorly. Treat them well and you may be surprised at what they can accomplish. It's so easy to acknowledge their work, their skill, their importance. How can any skipper do less? Without these incredible men and women, your hotshot ship would be a powerless barge stuck in the sand.

It took a while for these perfectly logical sentiments to pierce my own scrambled-egg cap. Like many captains, I was just as glad to leave engineering to the engineers. Looking under the ship's hood wasn't what interested me. The open-air world of combat systems and ship driving was my forte. I let engineering skills slide.

But the loss of power in San Diego Harbor had shaken us all. So early on we decided to set aside sufficient daylight time to allow the engineers to get the maximum benefit from their own training. It was a trade-off: the ship might have to settle for only 99 percent of its possible performance in combat operations, but engineering would rise from its 50 percent rating to 80 percent. The revised schedule also gave me the chance to observe the engineers' training and show a personal interest in what they were doing.

The department had 110 people, a little more than one third of the entire crew, and they controlled all of the ship's core systems. They included electricians, mechanics, generator operators, damage-control teams, even the person who runs the ship's sewage system—and each and every one of them had to be brought up to speed on how to respond quickly and intelligently to every possible contingency.

We developed a mind-boggling sequence of exercises designed to keep identifying, and mastering, worst-case scenarios so as to make it virtually certain we could handle anything less. To test an engineer's alertness on watch, for instance, we programmed a computer to order a sudden plunge in the oil pressure of one of the main engines. If the operator failed to notice and respond correctly, the whole power plant would shut down automatically. (Of course, as a precautionary measure, other people were forewarned and ready to prevent any shutdown. Had a major power fluctuation actually occurred—say, when the radar system was operating—the damage could have been horrendous.) All this training was tedious and time-consuming, but everyone agreed that it was the ship's first priority.

One immediate payoff was the discovery that the engineers doing the training were highly skilled operators, but lousy trainers. After they were shown how to improve their teaching skills, the engineering department progressed in giant leaps. We didn't have bad people, just bad processes. Soon we began working toward the ideal situation in which nearly every specialist would have a backup who could do his or her job in the event of illness, accident, transfer, or other sudden change. It was equivalent to doubling our expertise, a process that steadily improved the crew's readiness for just about anything.

A memorable reward for all our hard work came several months later when we were being graded on an anchorage exercise off San Diego. This is an operation performed in open water. You pick a point on your chart and see how close you can come to dropping your anchor on that precise spot. It's a major test of seamanship and navigation, requiring knowledge and understanding of wind, tide, the local currents, and the characteristics of your ship. The exercise is so demanding that if a ship successfully approaches an anchorage, it's taken for granted that it can also perform all the lesser mooring tasks, such as maneuvering into a slip or tying up alongside another ship.

As you approach your chosen anchorage, you disengage the propellers about five hundred yards out and float a little past the spot on momentum. Then you back into the spot very slowly because if you are moving forward when the anchor bites, it can damage the sonar dome. Bearing in mind the wind blowing in one direction and the tide moving you in another, the current at the surface and the contrary current fifty feet down, the depth of the water and how fast the anchor will drop, you let it go. Ideally, it will hit bottom within twenty-five yards of the chosen spot. You stop the chain and let the anchor dig into the bottom; then you snug up the chain, set the stoppers to hold it hard, and turn off your engines, safely moored.

But before you reach the anchorage, you have to prepare the anchor for letting go. The anchor is huge—*Benfold's* weighed ten thousand pounds—and the chain holding it is a lethal string of football-size links, each weighing forty pounds. The chain is divided into fifteen-foot segments called shots that are painted different colors near the end to indicate the number of links left in the anchor locker as the chain is paid out. The next-to-last shot is yellow and the last is red, which you don't want to ever see because it signals trouble: the chain is out so far that it may foul the ship's hull, or worse yet, break its last link and burst out of the anchor locker with enough force to decapitate anyone in the vicinity.

When the ship is under way, the anchor is secured by several sets of brakes and stoppers to make sure it doesn't accidentally let go. But as you prepare to drop anchor, all these fail-safe devices come off, one by one, until only the main brake on the anchor chain is left.

On this occasion, we were about fifteen hundred yards from the anchorage and steaming at fifteen knots when the main brake failed and the anchor let go. I was watching from the bridge as the anchor suddenly plunged into the water, the chain whipping out behind it. I immediately ordered the helmsman to reverse all engines at full speed to avoid a crash. But the chain was still hurtling out of the locker, and a runaway red end could kill someone as it left the ship.

Relentless training saved us. This was a freak accident, but we had rehearsed what to do. When I gave the order to reverse the engines, everyone leaped in and did his or her job. The helmsman followed my order instantly, and the engineers below prepared to complete the maneuver manually if the automatic controls broke down. *Benfold* reversed so quickly that the anchor, still dropping, was now ahead of us instead of under the ship.

The man who stopped the anchor was the chief boatswain's mate Scott Moede, a big, hardworking, and likable fellow with forearms like Popeye's. Moede ran up right beside the anchor locker and started cranking the manual wheel that acts as an emergency brake. The chain was flying out at fifteen to twenty feet per second, making an awful racket, and Moede was spinning the wheel furiously, with his eyes primed for yellow. The first yellow link was only three or four seconds from emerging when the brake grabbed hold, the chain slowed, and disaster was averted.

Moede was the hero of the day. But even more important, the situation was saved because everyone, including our engineers, knew exactly what to do and did it automatically. Apart from the clatter made by the flying chain, there was dead silence on the ship as everyone concentrated on following the scenario we had rehearsed. And besides saving the anchor and the chain, we prevented the sonar dome under the fo'c'sle from being crushed as the chain ran wild. My commodore was so astonished that navy divers were sent out to investigate our feat, confirming that the ship had suffered no damage. There was really nothing to investigate. It was all thanks to forethought, discipline, and training.

On my ship, success sprang from the magic of motivating ordinary people to buy into a good cause, give it their best shot, and thereby produce extraordinary results. The chief lesson was clear and simple: once your people really know something cold, they become proprietary about it and strive to perform with excellence. My crew became so possessive that they busted their butts to make *Ben-*

fold the best ship in the entire U.S. Navy. Given where they started, it was miracle enough that they made her—by official citation—the finest ship in the Pacific Fleet.

Could our experience be repeated elsewhere? It could and is: every single day hundreds of thousands of people in our armed forces deliver phenomenal performances. Having already published one book about my navy past, I decided there was a lot more to say about leadership in organizations of all kinds, not just the military. I began collecting examples from both military and civilian fields. Soon I discovered that the most refreshing leadership examples involved not the grossly overpaid corporate CEOs whose names dominate the headlines, but, rather, unsung leaders, remarkable people with remarkable stories that never receive the media hype. I hope you will like these people as much as I do. For one thing, their high performance is invariably leavened with self-effacing charm and a lack of pretense, which means they are easy to identify with. They could be us, and vice versa.

What follows is a series of lessons distilled from their experiences and mine. Each chapter briefly introduces one of these exemplary people, then explores his or her most interesting leadership insights and how they came to perceive them. Here's a quick rundown of the unsung leaders I want you to meet.

- Buddy Gengler, age twenty-six, went to Iraq in March of 2003, just as the war began. A West Point graduate and first lieutenant in the U.S. Army, Buddy was no stranger to hard work and trying times. But shortly after his arrival in the Middle East, he was confronted with an unexpectedly harrowing challenge: deployed to lead a platoon of rocket launchers, Buddy discovered that the soldiers under his command would, instead, be used as a street-fighting quick-reaction force—an extremely dangerous job for which they had received scant training. In chapter 1, you'll learn how Buddy met an extreme test of leadership while earning the respect of both his soldiers and his superiors.

- Trish Karter, forty-seven, is cofounder and chief executive of Dancing Deer Baking Company, headquartered in one of Boston's poorest areas. I discovered Dancing Deer while living in Boston. I love its products and became intrigued with the company itself and what makes it so special after I started doing a little digging. Trish switched her career from fine arts to business in order to help people in need. First, when her father's company was being reorganized under Chapter 11 proceedings, she dropped out of Wheaton College and worked side by side with him to get the company back on its feet. Then, when Suzanne Lombardi, the operator of a small bakery Trish and her husband had invested in, got overextended, Trish jumped in. Now Dancing Deer is nationally famous for its distinctive line of all-natural cakes and cookies that munchers find as sinfully tasty as they are environmentally pure. Result: Dancing Deer currently grosses $5 million a year, with annual sales rising rapidly. That's not all: Trish Karter and colleagues give away almost 10 percent of their revenues (that's not a misprint) to the bakery's needy neighbors. For more on Trish Karter's capitalistically incorrect enterprise and what we can learn from it, see chapter 2.

- Roger Valine is a fifty-five-year-old sociologist turned chief executive whose old-fashioned respect and concern for his employees has helped make Vision Service Plan, a Sacramento, California-based benefits provider, a paragon of civilized employer-employee relations. In these days of outsourcing and 24/7 workplaces, Roger sees no reason why a company man can't also be a family man, and he encourages his employees to follow his example by providing the kind of perks and benefits that make life easier and help stabilize families. But that doesn't mean he's a pushover for poor performance. On the contrary, Roger demands top-notch performance from every member of his crew and gets it: under his leadership, VSP has gone from a $500 million regional company to a national organization with over $2 billion in sales, and growing. In chapter 3, you'll learn more about the clear-eyed vision of Roger Valine and VSP.

- My friend Captain Al Collins, now forty-eight, was raised poor and black in rural Georgia and enlisted in the U.S. Navy in 1972. Al stood out from the start, rising rapidly to chief petty officer and handling many duties normally reserved for commissioned officers. He took college courses in his off-duty hours and was commissioned as an officer in a special program. He rose to be skipper of two U.S. Navy warships, one of which, USS *Fitzgerald,* like USS *Benfold* before it, won the coveted Spokane Trophy as the most battle-ready ship in the whole Pacific Fleet. Al went on to serve on the Iraq crisis action team of the Joint Chiefs of Staff, preparing the briefs for President George W. Bush on the daily progress of the war. He is one of the best men I've ever known, and a model for leaders everywhere, as you will see in chapter 4.

- Laura Folse, the forty-five-year-old vice president of technology for BP PLC, is a rarity in the decidedly male-dominated world of petroleum and gas exploration. But then Laura has been traveling the unbeaten path since she was a girl growing up in small-town Alabama. Freed by her parents from the typical limits placed on women in that place and time, she worked and studied alongside boys and men from an early age. Her intelligence and hard work earned Laura degrees in geology from Auburn University and the University of Alabama, and one in management from Stanford. It takes more than brainpower to succeed, however, and Laura has shown an uncommon talent for a gutsy yet compassionate style of leadership that makes her a standout at BP. "There's nothing better than working with a group of people toward a common goal," Laura told me, and in chapter 5, she shares her methods and philosophy for creating superior cohesive teams.

- Ward Clapham, age forty-five, joined the Royal Canadian Mounted Police in 1980. From his first assignment in an isolated backwater in Northern Alberta to his current job as superintendent of the 215-member detachment in the British Columbia city of Richmond, Ward has shown a natural bent for leadership and community interaction. When the Mounties took an official interest in the community policing philosophy back in 1991, Clapham was an early convert and eloquent proselytizer. He has lectured on the topic across three continents and is the author of several related articles. As Ward will tell you, though, no community can be successfully integrated into police work until the leader gains the buy in and respect of the men and women under his or her command. Chapter 6 relates the techniques Ward has used working with those fabled Mounties in a series of operations across Canada.

Now let's weigh anchor and sail at flank speed into the amazing sea of my favorite unsung leaders.

CHAPTER 1

First Lieutenant Buddy Gengler Calls for Help and Saves His Troops

*Your platoon is dumped in the middle of a war zone with
inadequate training for its assigned mission. What do you do?
You bust your butt to make sure this small band
of brothers survives.*

WHAT DOES A LEADER LOOK LIKE? WE ALL HAVE OUR OWN preconceived notions. For some people, it's easy to envision the Arnold Schwarzenegger action-oriented person as a leader. Others may unconsciously look for clues that bespeak status—expensive shoes, a good haircut, and well-tailored clothes made of good fabric. But in the U.S. military, where shoes and haircuts and uniforms are all the same, another indicator noted in certain studies on the topic may be the most reliable of all: a steady gaze. We Americans value a gaze that seems to absorb and process everything in sight (and quite a few things that aren't).

I thought about this tricky business of recognizing a leader while watching a homemade DVD sent by First Lieutenant Gabriel J. "Buddy" Gengler III. Made up of still photos and movies taken of Gengler and others in his army unit, it depicts his tour of duty in Iraq—from the time he crossed the berm from Kuwait and rode across the desert to Baghdad, all the way to his return stateside. In the twelve months from March 2003 to March 2004, Buddy captured scenes of tent life, sandstorm-riddled convoys, nighttime rocket attacks, military engagements on the streets of Baghdad, soldiers' softball games, visits with Iraqi schoolchildren, and much more. It's a 360-degree view of the war that TV news can't duplicate.

But for the first three or four minutes of the video, I couldn't pick out Buddy. Scenes moved too fast in the blur of soldiers in desert camouflage for me to identify rank or read a name tag. At that point, I hadn't yet met Buddy in person, and I knew him only through our correspondence. I'd heard tales of his successes as a military leader and the techniques he'd used to build a cohesive fighting unit after he read *It's Your Ship*. Maybe part of me was looking for that tall football-hero type, or maybe his exploits had given me a mental picture of a much older, more hard-bitten figure. For whatever reason, I didn't spot Buddy Gengler until I really started looking at faces. Then, suddenly, Buddy came into focus—a young spark plug of a guy with a steady gaze, the look of a leader.

And what a leader he is: deployed to Iraq to lead a platoon trained to fire a multiple-launch rocket system, Buddy soon discovered that the army planned instead to use his unit as a street-fighting, quick-reaction force to chase down bad guys, round up illegal weapons, and battle terrorists and insurgents in more than eight major operating locations spanning from Iraq's eastern border near Iran, to the northeast, and across central Iraq. Never mind that neither he nor his troops had received more than the most basic of training for this kind of combat. In the army you can't pick your missions.

Buddy didn't complain or throw up his hands; he just went to work putting his men through simulated raid after raid to build their instincts and improve their chances of surviving what lay ahead. In the end, Buddy's platoon earned a reputation as one of the most successful strike forces around, especially when it came to seizing caches of illegal weapons. Miraculously, not one member of the unit was lost or even seriously injured.

In this chapter are several stories of how Buddy protected his men, won their respect, helped them excel, and rewarded their success.

Thinking about Buddy Gengler, I have to wonder how often great leaders initially go unnoticed or unappreciated just because they don't fit the prevailing stereotype. I've been guilty of it myself. My heart sank the first time I met my executive officer on *Benfold,* Lieutenant Commander Jeff Harley (sorry, Jeff). We were among six prospective captains and six prospective executive officers going through the Aegis weapons training course together. It's a four-week course designed to train captains and executive officers for their demanding duties. If I had been told to choose any of the six to be my executive officer, Jeff wouldn't have made the cut. Here was the guy who was going to be my right-hand man, and he didn't look at all like the type you'd pick for football talk over a beer at the corner bar. Mild mannered and bespectacled, he resembled a professor more than a salty seaman. I had a hard time seeing myself teamed with someone so different from me.

The executive officer is sort of the ship's vice president. It's up to the captain to decide if that VP will be weak or strong—a Dan Quayle or a Dick Cheney. If your XO has the right stuff to wield influence, that's a force multiplier for the captain. If not, well, at least you've got someone to handle administrative duties.

Jeff arrived on USS *Benfold* three months before me because I still had more training to complete. I had immediately judged him to be the administrative type, so my first inclination was to keep him pigeonholed. But before I made that snap decision, I decided to call a close friend, Captain Dallas Bethea, for whom Jeff had previously served on USS *Cowpens* as operations officer. My first inclination could not have been more wrong. Dallas had nothing but wonderful things to say about Jeff, and his glowing report opened my closed mind just a bit. I am forever grateful to Dallas for that.

When I allowed my mind to open up completely, what I saw changed my entire perception of Jeff. He had the answer to every question I asked, even ones I myself had had to look up back when I was an executive officer. He knew minute details of *Benfold*'s operations and demonstrated an encyclopedic grasp of information about my fellow commanders—which ones were already in the Middle East; which ones, like us, would be deployed soon; and how each of them liked to operate. I had been out of the region and out of the loop for three years, so Jeff's knowledge saved me enormous time and legwork.

Any remaining doubt about whether this rather unassuming man could be an active and influential executive officer who would command the respect of the crew was shortly laid to rest. Jeff had a wonderful way about him that made everyone more than happy to follow him—he was likable and genuine, not to mention technically competent. The crew would bust a gut for Jeff. All he had to do was ask.

In his earlier days as an officer, Jeff had served on USS *David R. Ray*, a destroyer that had a nasty habit of flunking its engineering certifications. Two chief engineers in a row had been fired before Jeff arrived as number three. At that point, he had no engineering background whatsoever. But he was a warm body with a pulse, which was enough to land him that job. Initially, I think, Jeff's new captain had also made a snap judgment about him. But being the tenacious sort, he just dug in and got to work, trying to learn everything he could about the job at hand.

One day the commanding officer called Jeff to say his cabin toilet wasn't working. Jeff was ordered to report to the head and stay there until it was fixed. Now the area in question was pretty cramped. Jeff ended up spending the whole day sitting on the CO's toilet, wheel book in his lap, looking up who was supposed to be doing what and when, and using the CO's phone to run the engineering department. (When Jeff describes this scene, he breaks everyone up.) After the needed parts finally arrived and the toilet was fixed, Jeff was set free at last—but only after the CO had test-driven his newly repaired toilet.

After hearing Jeff's story, no one would turn down a chance to work with him—me included.

Jeff Harley turned around the engineering department on *David R. Ray* and parlayed that achievement into two promotions that brought him to *Benfold*. Given his depth of knowledge, experience, and leadership skills, I was only too happy to make him both my number-one administrator and my number-two war fighter. It was a decision that paid off enormously, as you'll soon see. But first, let me share with you some of the leadership lessons I discovered in my conversations with Buddy Gengler.

LESSON: Call in the reserves when you need them.

Like any good leader, First Lieutenant Buddy Gengler gives full credit to his troops for their top-notch performance in Iraq. They couldn't have done it without him, of course, but he doesn't let the kudos obscure a hard truth: there are many things Buddy Gengler doesn't know, such as how to turn a band of rocket launchers into a quick-reaction force. One of his great strengths is his willingness—determination, even—to look for outside expertise.

If that kernel of wisdom seems too obvious to make a fuss over, ask yourself how often you've heard a leader say, "I'm not smart enough to do a real good job of teaching you how to do this. I'm going to find somebody smarter." Because that, in effect, is what Buddy Gengler told his soldiers when they unexpectedly had to take on an entirely new and very dangerous assignment in Iraq.

Truth telling takes guts. It also takes a high level of self-confidence and a willingness to be seen as less than the all-knowing leader—two things many people in authority do not possess. The irony is that underlings can sense that fear of exposure, and once they do, they lose respect for their leaders. By contrast, having the courage to admit ignorance and the wisdom to seek help, as Buddy did, wins the admiration of those you command.

As soon as Buddy learned of his platoon's recalibrated mission, he set out to find someone with solid experience in what the army calls MOUT, military operations in urban terrain. A ranger-trained officer in Buddy's battalion who fit the bill agreed to put the platoon through the necessary exercises, teaching the soldiers how to cover for others under enemy fire and similar combat techniques.

On their first day as quick responders, while nervously awaiting news of a flare-up that would require them to take action, Buddy took the opportunity to talk about how platoon members should process any prisoners. He had received some training at West Point but was far from expert. Waiting alongside Buddy's platoon were the operators of the Bradley armored transport vehicles. One of the Bradley operators was noticeably listening in, so Buddy asked if he had anything to add. It turned out the man was a former marine MP who had dealt with war prisoners. He gladly pitched in with first-rate advice on how to restrain prisoners, make sure they weren't carrying weapons or explosives, and handle their belongings.

The marine had barely finished when the order came to move in. Buddy's platoon was soon pouring out of the Bradleys on a street corner under siege. "Adrenaline was rushing, shots were being fired," he recalled, "and I saw my soldiers immediately do a job perfectly that they had never done before. It absolutely blew my mind." When the firefight subsided, Buddy's platoon counted thirty-eight prisoners and more than fifty weapons, including mortars, taken in its first mission. Best of all, nobody in the platoon was even injured.

For Buddy, the experience of that first mission reinforced something he already knew: "When there are ideas or expert reference power around you, you've got to be able and willing to use it. I couldn't and wouldn't do anything else in Iraq with my soldiers' lives on the line, but it goes beyond that. A lot of leaders I've been around in other much less dangerous situations were not willing to [ask for help]. They put their own pride first. It's a big mistake."

I battled my own vanity one dark night in January of 1998 when *Benfold* was tracking an Iraqi smuggler down the coast of Iran. It turned out to be the one and only night when I was, by necessity, not in command of the situation.

We were looking for a 125-to-150-foot Iraqi ship, a minitanker of sorts, that was smuggling fuel oil to avoid the sanctions placed on Saddam Hussein by the United Nations. Typically, these outlaws offloaded their oil at a port in the United Arab Emirates. After leaving Iranian territorial waters near the Strait of Hormuz, it was only about a ten-mile jaunt through international waters into UAE territory.

That's where the cat-and-mouse game of trying to intercept a smuggler's ship was played.

On this particular night we knew exactly where the smuggler was, but we didn't know when he was going to leave Iranian waters and make his dash for the UAE. When he suddenly made his move, *Benfold* and a British cruiser were ordered to give chase.

I ran to the bridge, knowing we had one chance, and one chance only, to get this guy. As I went topside to oversee things amid all the confusion, I found myself positively blinded. I had no idea where we were in relation to land and couldn't see a thing because of a full moon and the paralyzing glare of background light from land and the other ships in the area. Until my eyes adjusted, I experienced a spatial disorientation that I had never felt before—like a pilot who can't tell air from water or stars from city lights. It must have been similar to the pilot's vertigo that in 1999 caused John F. Kennedy Jr. to accidentally plunge his plane into the Atlantic waters off the coast of Massachusetts near Martha's Vineyard.

Making matters worse was the anxiety I felt. It was my job to catch that smuggler before he escaped into UAE waters, which he could do in less than thirty minutes. Each passing second of disorientation made me more panicky, and the more I panicked, the longer it took to reorient myself.

Finally, I realized I needed help, so I swallowed my pride and turned to Jeff Harley, my XO. "It's your baby," I told him. "You've got the conn"—meaning that he had control over *Benfold*'s maneuvering. "Take responsibility . . . because I can't right now."

Night vision is crucial when you're navigating a ship, and you don't always have the couple of minutes it takes for your eyes to adjust to the dark. The navy tries to counteract the problem by installing red lights in cabins and passageways. After dark, the white lights go down and the red ones come up. I usually spent evenings in my cabin under very subdued red lights just in case I had to go up to the bridge. That way, my eyes would adjust quickly.

On this particular night I had been doing just that. Ironically, I was too well prepared for the dark. The full moon and the glare from the land made the outside world a lot brighter than I had expected—certainly brighter than my cabin. Jeff had been on the bridge for hours, so he was fine. I wasn't happy at being temporarily incapacitated and unable to lead at that moment, but I was proud to have such a worthy leader to fill in for me. It was unconventional to turn over command to my executive officer—it was the first and last time I had to let someone else take charge. But it was absolutely the right thing to do.

I'd like to be able to end the story by saying that Jeff performed flawlessly and we caught the smuggler, but that would be only half right. Jeff did perform flawlessly, but the smuggler got away. The only way we could have stopped the guy was to ram him, and we weren't going to risk a billion-dollar ship on a rust bucket. So the British cruiser started firing warning shots at the smuggler. Unfortunately, *Benfold* was in the line of fire on the other side. I thought of picking up the phone and saying to the Brits, "I surrender, so stop shooting at us." But I didn't want to be the first modern U.S. warship to surrender to the Brits—even in jest. We had little choice but to drop back and watch the smuggler steam off to bootleg another day.

When I think back on incidents like that one, I thank my lucky stars that I had the good sense not to judge Jeff Harley on first impressions. Fortunately, I took the time to see not only who he was, but who he could be. In a host of small and not-so-small ways, I groomed my XO for the authority I wanted him to be able to assume. Leaders owe it to their organizations to prepare others for command. If we were refueling from an oiler, for example, I would turn to him for advice on our position. In public, when others were watching and waiting for me to make a decision, I'd turn to Jeff and say, "What do you think?" In these ways, I increased Jeff's stature on the ship. Saying he was second in command wasn't enough; I had to live those words every day if I wanted the crew to believe that Jeff was, in fact, my right-hand man.

I put my faith in writing too. The glowing evaluations I wrote for Jeff helped him get his own ship, USS *Milius,* which has become the best destroyer based in San Diego. What did I say in those evaluations? Simply that Jeff Harley was the best officer I had observed in my entire career. And that's true. He has now been selected for full-bird captain and will command his own cruiser. And what is more, I would have a beer with him any day.

LESSON: Dare your crew to be the best, and they will deliver.

Have you ever noticed how a lot of folks seem to divide the world into two kinds of people, a small group of serious overachievers, which naturally includes themselves, and a large majority of slackers, those doing the very minimum to get by? In the view of the overachievers, the slackers simply accept their fate and put in their time on some menial job. They may bitch and moan, but it won't do them any good. After all, they have no special talents and little or no ambition. All of that resides in the achiever class.

Fair warning: if you espouse this worldview and behave accordingly toward the people under your command, you will create a self-fulfilling prophecy—and you and your company will be the worse for it. Why? Because enormous energy and inventiveness lie fallow within some of those so-called slackers, just waiting to be activated by a leader who will challenge and inspire them to step out and accept greater responsibility.

Sure there's risk, both for you and for the people you push ahead— failure can be embarrassing and frustrating. But, believe me, the rewards far outweigh the downside.

Buddy Gengler has seen it go both ways. He has dared others to prove themselves, and been dared himself. He has seen some people rise to meet his expectations, and some fall short. But out of it all has emerged a champion of the challenge process who has notched numerous victories on his belt. Indeed, the order Buddy most enjoys giving contains just four words: "You are in charge."

As the leader of a platoon charged with firing a multiple-launch rocket system, Buddy's primary battle task was to perform forward reconnaissance and ensure a safe operating area (meaning no enemy are present) for the launchers to move ahead. In convoys, Gengler's vehicle was always first, in front of even his commanders, and it was equipped with its own weapon system, a gunner, and a sergeant who drove. The sergeant was also responsible for making sure that both the vehicle and weapon system were in good repair, and that his soldiers were always ready for any contingency mission.

Buddy gave the sergeant so-so marks—a good soldier but far from outstanding in the performance of his not-very-demanding duties. The vehicle wasn't always ready when needed; the ammunition can occasionally went missing from its place beside the weapon system; a dirty windshield often clouded Buddy's view—not an ideal situation for an officer on reconnaissance. "The sergeant should have been better at his job," Buddy told me. But then Buddy added: "I don't think he was challenged by it."

So Buddy found him a challenge.

When the platoon was reassigned to street-fighting duty shortly after arriving in Iraq, Buddy had to split the platoon in half to cover a twenty-four-hour period. He planned to lead one group himself and had a platoon sergeant in mind to lead the other. But first Buddy had to find someone to handle the platoon sergeant's substantial and complex duties at the operating base, which entailed getting food, water, and everything else to soldiers in the field so that they could operate at peak efficiency. The replacement would also have to guarantee round-the-clock security, since the base was vulnerable to attack at any moment.

Thinking that his lackadaisical sergeant-driver had unrealized potential, Buddy asked him to assume the role of acting platoon sergeant. "I know this is not your job," Buddy told him, "but I need you to take it on and make sure everything is going right back here so I can focus on getting ready for the next mission."

Buddy was not disappointed. Within days, the base was operating smoothly. In fact, supplies started arriving at their destinations earlier and weapons and vehicles were cleaner and in better repair—all this from a guy who couldn't seem to maintain just one vehicle only a short time before. Suddenly, the sergeant was "walking around with a new air of confidence I'd never seen," Buddy said. "His reputation within the platoon changed completely."

The nearly miraculous thing was the effect the temporary platoon sergeant had on the rest of the team, whose morale had been devastatingly low. Mail was arriving irregularly if at all, water was so scarce that the soldiers marked lines on their water bottles to ration it, and the troops were being subjected to broiling temperatures. When they returned from a patrol, drenched in sweat and exhausted, the only thing most wanted to do was sack out. But, somehow, the sergeant, having taken complete responsibility for his own job, managed to motivate the soldiers to do the same. He had them cleaning their weapons and otherwise staying in a state of readiness for a possible attack. There's nothing like a new convert to inspire the masses.

The sergeant's amazing performance would never have happened if Buddy had not given him a chance to excel. He challenged the sergeant to reach higher than he'd ever reached before, and the sergeant rose to the occasion. That sergeant has since gone on to win a promotion.

Once a leader recognizes someone's potential to do more, Buddy said, it's the leader's duty to help the underachiever excel. The former slacker may be embarrassed or nervous about being out in front, and it's up to the leader to supply the confidence the person needs to step up.

As I mentioned, Buddy has been on both ends of the challenge. His commanding officer asked him to take over the quick-response duties after he came to Iraq primed for another mission. But Buddy didn't hesitate, even though he was being asked to move outside his area of expertise. He was ready and eager to learn something new and to assume a larger leadership role, which, in itself, is the mark of a great leader.

"It was a gutsy call," he said of the CO's decision to place an inexperienced young officer in the role. "It might not have worked out. In business, if you make a bad decision, you lose money. You make a bad decision in the military—you put somebody on a post at the wrong time or the wrong place—and the next thing you know, you're writing a letter to their parents."

But in or out of the military, challenging your team members to take on larger roles is a vital and necessary part of leading and of forging new leaders. For Buddy, the commanding officer's decision to widen his responsibilities changed his life. "Because he gave me those experiences, now whatever I'm faced with as a leader," Buddy said, "I have a bedrock confidence because I know nothing will be more difficult than what I achieved in Iraq." And because of what was done for him, he has become more willing to delegate power and trust to his soldiers. "I know full well that it's my shoes that will be smoking in front of my superior's desk if it doesn't work out," he said, "but I will do it because that's what good leaders do."

I did a similar thing on *Benfold* when I allowed all qualified watch standers, regardless of rank, to have access to the radio telephones—the ship-to-ship receiving-and-transmitting radio system that allows members of a carrier battle group to communicate with one another. Previously, only officers could use the R/T nets on *Benfold*. But I thought every watch stander should have access to ship-to-ship communication links if his or her duties required it.

However, I was extremely demanding about what was said. No one on my ship was going to key the microphone and say something dumb, such as "Hey *Nimitz,* this is Bob here on *Benfold.*" Of all the traditions that I sought to uphold, speaking clearly and concisely on the R/T net was the one with no room for compromise. I expected superior performance from everyone. You represented USS *Benfold* every time you keyed that radio, so you had better know exactly what you were going to say beforehand.

The captain's cabin on *Benfold* was its own little nerve center. I could watch the radar, monitor the flight deck, and, yes, tune in to the R/T nets. I had rigged up extra circuits (contrary to navy regulations, actually) so I could monitor conversations on three radios at the same time. And if I heard something I didn't like, something that didn't sound polished and professional, I was swift and merciless. Keying up my intercom, I'd simply intone my displeasure, sounding like the voice of God.

No one ever did anything awful. But they didn't always put *Benfold*'s best foot forward. You know how a flight attendant will sometimes key the microphone on a plane, having every intention of saying something intelligent, only to end up sounding like a complete idiot—with all the passengers snickering? That's what happened to some of my crew members. I remember one in particular, a fantastic sonar technician named Drew Martinez. Great as he was at tracking submarines, he had not been trained to be a gifted communicator. When speaking on the net, he went on and on and round and round, taking far too long to get where he wanted to go. That's when I would break in and share my displeasure. "Chief Martinez," I'd intone, "I was not impressed with your last transmission." Sailors sitting at their consoles with headsets dreaded hearing the captain come on to critique their transmissions publicly. And, normally, I was not one to criticize publicly. However, the outside world forms its opinion of your organization based on your spokespeople. I wanted those watch standers to know they were our spokespeople.

Clear, crisp, and concise professional communication is an indicator of your commitment to your job. I believe that if you pay attention to the way you communicate, the chances are good that you're also paying attention to every other aspect of your work. Poor communication is not an absolute indicator of other job-related problems, but often, once you start connecting the dots, you do discover other areas that need work. Sloppy speaking habits were one of my pet peeves, and, interestingly enough, my crew soon felt the same way. Martinez eventually became a first-rate R/T net communicator, and he was only too happy to join the rest of the crew in heckling other ships when their messages were unclear or just plain stupid.

In their heart of hearts, however, my sailors apparently still wished I'd quit hassling them. Here's how I know: The bridge kept a top-ten list of most-favorite and least-favorite words and phrases employed by their dear captain, me. Right at the top of the favorites was my nightly request on the intercom: "Bridge, would you please turn down the volume on my radios?" That told them that I was going to sleep and wouldn't be listening for a few hours. The ship would breathe a collective sigh of relief. The least favorite phrase? "Bridge, would you please turn up the volume on my radios?" That meant that it was a new day and the captain was listening again.

LESSON: Don't rush to judgment.

Maybe you've heard it said that the shit always rolls downhill? Nowhere is this truer than in the military. Whenever an admiral, general, or captain is upset about something, the second in command is the one to catch hell, followed by the department heads, and, last but not least, the enlisted men get the hot seat. Rarely does a higher-up stop the cascade to ask, "Gee, what really happened here? Exactly why did things go so wrong?"

As the dutiful product of my training, I joined the officers' corps able to kick butt and take names with the best of them. But during sixteen years in jobs on land and at sea, I gradually learned to quit shouting expletives and start asking questions. Time and experience taught me what should have been obvious: if I didn't get the results I wanted, either I didn't clearly articulate what we were trying to do, or I didn't provide the time, training, and resources to do the job properly. When I finally stopped yelling and began probing for answers, though, I was surprised that people actually became uncomfortable. That's because abusive behavior toward underlings is indelibly ingrained in the military. When you don't do it, nobody knows quite how to respond. But when they begin to trust that problems will be handled with respect and an open mind, the atmosphere improves noticeably—and even poor performers begin to succeed.

For me, the light dawned when I realized that I was dealing with some very fine, smart people whose goals and standards were just like mine. Some had hidden skills or talents, like a waiter you meet in a restaurant who turns out to be finishing his dissertation for the London School of Economics. Others came from disadvantaged backgrounds, but had the brains and energy to achieve great success. No one, least of all a leader, should write someone off based on stereotypes or the person's station in life.

On *Benfold*, I learned that everyone has a story, and my job as commander was to know as many of those stories as possible. Not only did that knowledge help me devise the right work assignment for each individual, it also helped me understand why things went wrong, as they inevitably did.

Over the years and with hard experience of my own, I realized that probably 80 percent of screwups aren't caused by lack of will or skill; rather, they're caused by something distracting the people who screw up. Everybody hits speed bumps in life. I went through a painful divorce in 1995, just before I went to *Benfold*, and some days it was hard to keep my mind on the job. I never missed a day of work, but I'm sure it affected my performance. Before that, I'd never understood how anybody could let a personal problem affect his professional life. It had never happened to me. But once it did, it changed me.

Now when I don't get the results I'm looking for from someone, I don't yell; I ask myself what I could have done differently. It never fails to throw everyone off—they're trying to figure out why I'm so quiet! And I'm always conscious of the possibility of an emotional component when someone fails to perform, anything from illness to financial stress to a personal upheaval like my divorce. Adversity definitely made me a better listener. It probably also made me a better person and a stronger leader.

It took Buddy Gengler about sixteen years to learn these lessons, but, unlike me, it wasn't sixteen years of his career. Some of his most indelible lessons about leadership were learned in the first sixteen years of his life.

Buddy was a sophomore in high school when his mother was diagnosed with cancer. She immediately told her husband and their seven children not to mention her illness to anyone. She didn't want sympathy from outsiders. During the months leading up to his mother's death, Buddy's grades plummeted. He was tired and listless—a star on the high school baseball team who suddenly couldn't field or hit. Teachers and students alike asked what was wrong, but he wouldn't go against his mother's wishes. There was talk of his being lazy, a loner, probably both.

One afternoon his baseball coach finally sat Buddy down, determined to find out what was troubling him. By this time, Buddy's mother was slipping into the end stage of her disease, and the poor kid could no longer keep his hurt inside. He broke down in tears as the tragic story spilled out. The coach wasted no time in visiting each of Buddy's teachers, explaining that every day the boy went directly home from school to sit by his mother's side. He wasn't sleeping at night. He couldn't concentrate on his schoolwork, on his baseball, on anything other than his mother. The coach appealed to the teachers, as Buddy remembered it, "to cut this guy some slack." They did.

After his mother's death, Buddy gradually began to recover his old self. He never forgot what the coach had done for him—or how easy it is to misjudge people on the basis of unexplained behavior.

"When a soldier falls asleep on guard duty or is underperforming," Buddy told me, "there is a whole host of possible reasons." Yes, he said, that soldier should be able to do better no matter what, but that's not the way life is. "People go into lulls," he went on. "They're not consistent. They're under stress from combat, or maybe because they called home and a strange voice answered. Before you lower the boom, look into it. You don't want to lose a good soldier over something temporary or fixable."

When someone is grappling with a hard situation, as Buddy pointed out, there are usually telling clues. Maybe a good soldier shows up late or unshaven and in a dirty uniform, or an excellent soldier turns in a mediocre report. When confronted, they may deny that anything's wrong because the situation is embarrassing or they don't want to appear weak. Buddy told me about a soldier whose performance was suffering because he was being hounded by creditors and losing sleep over it. He couldn't do anything about it because the credit office was closed by the time he left work. All the guy needed was a weekday off to straighten out his financial problems, but he was too proud to ask.

Usually, it takes some insistent prodding—and an open mind to frame nonaccusing questions—from a person in authority to get the real story. "The way I was raised," Buddy said, "was to think that if you're not doing your job, it's a character flaw. I still have to fight myself not to leap to judgment." And like most of us, he sometimes falls short, as when he came down hastily and hard on his soldiers at Fort Hood, Texas, where Buddy was stationed from January 2002 until October 2003.

A colonel happened to see some of Buddy's platoon members throwing a basketball around during a physical training period. The colonel jumped on Buddy's major for allowing his men to play an organized sport when they were supposed to be doing push-ups, sit-ups, chin-ups, and the like. The major immediately cornered Buddy, demanding to know why he had allowed this clear violation of base rules. Buddy, in turn, immediately dressed down his troops: What kind of numskulls would be playing basketball during PT? Hadn't the no-organized-sports rule been in place roughly since creation? How could these men forget something so incredibly basic?

When Buddy paused to catch his breath, one of the men managed to get a word in edgewise. Turns out they were not playing an outlawed basketball game at all. To liven up an otherwise boring PT session, they had added an extra wrinkle to the routine: a soldier who tried to shoot a basket and missed had to run an extra distance and do a specified number of additional sit-ups and push-ups.

Buddy felt awful for flying off the handle. "They were wrong to even fool around with a basketball," Buddy said, "but I assumed they were simply violating a rule they knew about and hoping to get away with it. I was as bad as the colonel, jumping to a conclusion and acting on it without checking my facts first. I wasted a lot of angry energy on something I didn't need to be angry about." Worse yet, Buddy missed an opportunity to build a better relationship with his platoon and risked losing their trust—all because he failed to get all the facts before he acted.

I once did something similar but worse. Six years later, I still feel bad about it.

Benfold was operating in the Persian Gulf, and we had spent several days in the midst of a fishing fleet dodging dhows. Avoiding collisions is just good seamanship, of course, but it is also seen as a security issue as well. The commanding officer of the aircraft carrier USS *John F. Kennedy* was relieved for cause in the summer of 2004 when his ship hit and sank a dhow. The small, sailboatlike dhows can be laden with explosives to blow up a ship. So whenever a dhow or any other small watercraft comes within four thousand yards, the bridge notifies the captain, who may opt to come to the bridge to monitor the situation.

Just before the incident I'm about to relate, I had been up and down the ladder to the bridge all night long, just overseeing all this zigging and zagging around dhows. I hadn't had any sleep. The next day, during man-overboard drills and preparation for possible missions later that day, I felt positively miserable. I had no patience whatsoever as I watched Oscar, our man-overboard dummy, get heaved over the side. Oscar was still in the water awaiting rescue when a call came directing us to search some Iraqi ships for contraband. You could almost see the smoke wafting from my ears—why couldn't we get this drill over with and get started on the mission?

It takes some very skillful maneuvering to reverse heading and bring a 505-foot ship about, particularly with the finesse and speed required to rescue a single person in a flotation device before hypothermia sets in. Every officer has to try his or her hand at it, and how long it takes to recover the dummy is a matter of pride. Everyone remembers his or her best time.

The junior officer who had the bad luck to be driving the boat when the orders came in that day wasn't going to set any records. She missed on the first pass, eating up an extra eight minutes to come around again. If there was a strategy behind what she was doing, I couldn't fathom it. The longer it took, the quieter she got, probably because she knew we needed to bug out as quickly as possible and her performance wasn't helping us any. Dead tired and short tempered, I was fuming. Before I knew it, I ripped into her: "I don't understand why anybody on this ship doesn't understand how to retrieve a man overboard. How frigging stupid can you be?"

Then I made things even worse by ordering that the commissioning pennant be hauled down. This pennant shows that the ship has been officially put in service, and every commissioned U.S. Navy ship on active duty flies one twenty-four hours a day. Hauling it down was the same as saying: "You guys are such an embarrassment, it's an embarrassment to even call this ship in commission." I had seen another captain do this once, and in my fatigue and irritation, I didn't have the sense to stop myself from pulling the same theatrical stunt.

She began to cry, and everyone on the bridge saw it. It didn't take more than a few seconds for me to realize that I had been way out of line, as childish and ineffectual as some jerk ranting and raving at an airline ticket counter. Throwing a fit doesn't work there, and it didn't work here either.

So I apologized. My junior officer's strategy for backing up the ship was unconventional and seemed to require more twisting of the ship than I thought necessary, but it would have worked. I could have seen that if I hadn't been so tired and impatient and I told her so.

Even good leaders sometimes do stupid things, especially when they're tired or under stress. If you've built a track record, and people know your outburst is out of the ordinary, they will give you the benefit of the doubt. But if you do it repeatedly, they will begin to disregard you even when you have a valid point to rant about. That's the fine line you walk when you throw temper tantrums.

For those of us who came to command through the 1980s and earlier, it's a long, hard slog to learn that the old methods aren't always the best methods. We have a saying in our community that we eat our young. For the life of me, I can't understand why we'd be proud of that. I decided it was past time to change it. We have to break out of our comfort zones, look around, and accept that all the evidence points to better results when we bark less and listen more. But the younger generation of military officers is breaking the code. Better training is helping the Buddy Genglers to become better leaders at a younger age. The military will be the better for it. Heck, it already *is* the better for it.

LESSON: Learn from your bad experiences.

One of the worst experiences of my navy career was also one of my best. I received the Ship Handler of the Year Award in 1983, a much-coveted prize for seamanship, and I did it in one of the least encouraging environments I could ever imagine.

Straight out of officers' school, I was assigned to an old rust bucket, USS *Albert David*. It was a frigate, a low-powered submarine-hunting class of ship devised in the 1960s mostly as a money saver. Believe me, you get what you pay for. But I didn't have much choice in the assignment. All the plums went to officers who had better grades at the Naval Academy, and I could either sit around waiting for something better to come out of overhaul or take *Albert David*. I didn't want to sit.

But just as the best junior officers go to the best ships, so do the best senior officers. Which meant that *Albert David* was not the first choice of the senior officers assigned there either. In fact, the environment was so belittling and downright abusive that most of the young guys didn't even want to drive the ship. There was no encouragement, no allowance for the occasional misjudgment. You'd be standing there with your engines on line as the micromanaging captain screamed orders in your ear that you were supposed to parrot. Or maybe he'd stand there totally silent, allowing you to make the calls, until some perceived miscue prompted a sudden stream of obscenities.

I didn't like it any better than anyone else, but I loved driving the ship, so I put up with it. If the criticism I got was justified, I took it. If not, I let it roll off my back. But operating in this high-pressure environment helped turn me into a very good ship driver. I became the go-to guy for taking *Albert David* in and out of port, and for the most difficult ship-handling maneuvers, as well.

That year, ten junior officers in the Pacific Fleet were named Ship Handlers of the Year. I was one of them and it was a tremendous honor. I probably owe that certificate, in part, to the crummy atmosphere on *Albert David*.

What I learned, though, is that leaders are also teachers, for better or worse. They teach us what not to do as well as what we should do. Even though I survived and succeeded in that environment, I vowed I would never emulate the abusive leadership styles. I've had to develop a style of management that better suited me and my sailors.

Buddy Gengler learned the same lesson as a cadet at West Point, where he cocaptained the baseball team. The coach treated his players like children. He was a micromanager who ordered the players around arbitrarily and refused to give the cocaptains any role in dealing with the rest of the team. He discouraged suggestions from the players and ignored those that came anyway. "I hated the way he led us," Buddy told me. "We played in spite of him; we played for each other."

But there was one thing Buddy liked. The coach encouraged a never-say-die attitude: "Challenge me. I will not give up. I will not succumb to any situation. I will not be afraid to be great." Some of the players were nervous about going to the plate when the game was on the line—bottom of the ninth, two outs, bases loaded. The coach would spur them on, insisting that these moments of peak challenge were life's greatest gifts and should be welcomed and sought out.

Today Buddy says, "I will eat up any challenge anyone puts in front of me"—and he owes his winning attitude in large measure to that baseball coach.

Like most of us, Buddy has thrived and suffered under the sway of more than one mediocre leader. His commanding officer at Fort Hood gave him plenty of examples of negative leadership, made ever so slightly more palatable by a positive note interjected here and there. For example, Buddy is quick to point out how grateful he is to this CO for giving him the chance to head up a new mission in Iraq. But by and large, he thinks the guy's behavior was a study in poor leadership.

"He could not deal with people," Buddy said. "He took no input from his subordinates on how things were going or how they should be done. He issued his orders, and that was it. He stifled initiative. To cap it all, he was rude and insolent, undermining junior leaders in front of our troops."

The morale of the battery sank so low that some soldiers were willing to leave their families behind and transfer just about anywhere to get away from him, Buddy said. Finally, Buddy went to see the CO after they'd had a major falling-out. He pulled no punches, telling him: "You have completely isolated all of your leadership, and people would rather leave this battery than have to see you every day." Buddy's comments were initially met with a blank stare. Then the CO became defensive, suggesting that his subordinates were less skilled and not as capable as he was of understanding the leadership role.

After that confrontation, the commander's attitude improved ever so slightly, Buddy said, but not nearly enough. The CO could still drive a soldier to despair—and did during the early days of the battery's tour in Iraq. Buddy told me about the day when one troubled young man nearly went over the edge.

Drained by the intense heat, a group of soldiers were sitting and talking casually when this fellow suddenly put a bullet in his weapon and stood up. "His eyes were red and wild looking," Buddy recalled. "Where you going, soldier?" Buddy asked him.

"I can't handle this anymore," he responded. "The commander represents everything that's going wrong in my life."

Buddy got the soldier to sit back down and hand over his weapon. When the kid began to talk, Buddy discovered that he was totally stressed out, partly from combat, partly because of things at home— his wife had had a miscarriage—but mainly because of the atmosphere the commander created in the battery. Buddy asked him, on a scale of one to ten, how close he was to actually doing something to the commanding officer.

The answer: "Nine."

When the soldier calmed down, Buddy went to the commander and told him he had come close to being assassinated by one of his own soldiers. Incredibly, this guy just shrugged his shoulders and sneered, "That's why I wear my protective vest."

He was so out of touch as a leader, Buddy said, that he didn't give a thought to his own role in a near tragedy. "He just assumed the problem was with the soldier."

But Buddy didn't let the incident pass. Showing his courage and the depth of his commitment to his platoon, Buddy contacted an army mental health team that was a ninety-minute drive from his base. The therapists agreed to examine conditions at the battery, interviewing individual soldiers about their attitudes toward the commander and their morale in general. The soldier whose distress inspired Buddy's efforts was soon evaluated and sent to a support base for a period of relaxation away from the combat zone. So grateful were Buddy's soldiers for the health team's intervention that some were choking back tears when they thanked him.

In the end, the therapists told the commanding officer many of the same things Buddy had told him. This time, however, he seemed to get the message and did improve his behavior toward the troops.

Buddy came away from this trying experience with a greater understanding of the huge impact leaders can have, for good or ill, on their followers. He could actually track the effect on his platoon of each arbitrary order from the CO, each refusal to listen to advice from his officers, each insult. It was not Buddy's first experience with poor leadership, but it was still an eye-opener.

LESSON: Know when to ignore the rules, and be prepared to take the heat.

Rules and regulations are the lifeblood of the American military. They form the basis of military discipline, which supports the authority of command. They also hamstring the service from time to time when rules are slavishly followed by people who lack the courage to be true leaders.

From what I can see, a lot of companies are like the military, filled with people who follow rules and never even think of doing anything else. There's no denying that rules and regulations can be a useful guide, and that they provide a sense of security. By telling us how *not* to behave and setting limits within which we can focus our minds and energies, they make our jobs easier. At the same time, we can feel secure knowing that, as long as we go by the book, we have a better chance of remaining employed, collecting a salary, and, if we're lucky, even cashing a monthly pension check one day.

The problem is that playing it safe is no way to run a company or a navy. The world is moving too fast, and there are too many occasions when trouble strikes and the best solution lies outside the stated boundaries. Countless opportunities have been lost because someone objected, "We don't do it that way around here." In fact, one definition of a great leader might very well be someone who has the capacity to choose the right moment to ignore the regulations and break new ground.

In my own career in the navy, I constantly tried to push the envelope, developing new approaches that went beyond the norm; if they stretched or exceeded my presumed command authority, so be it. Each time, of course, I risked falling flat on my face—and sometimes I did end up with a bruise or two. But on balance, the positives, for me and for the navy, far outweighed the negatives.

I didn't start out so willing to bend rules, though. That ability grew with time, experience, and especially the pointed words of my first commodore, Pat Slattery. Slattery had barely gotten to know me when he had to produce my first fitness report. He'd been off on a deployment for six weeks, then a vacation, and, all of a sudden, it was two weeks till my first evaluation was due. Some people might consider it a dream job to be working and never see the boss, but not me. I knew that of the six commanders he was supervising, Slattery would almost certainly rank me sixth. What else could he do? I was new on the job, and he'd barely crossed paths with me.

As I expected, my evaluation was lousy. I was ranked six of six, but I let Slattery know that I intended to be number one next time around. The commodore was not a chummy man, and most of us could never figure him out. But he barked out a simple piece of advice that changed the way I look at rules and regulations. Slattery told me, "If you want to be ranked first, then take command. That's what I pay you for. Don't expect me to do your job for you."

He went on to gripe that the other captains in the squadron brought all their problems to him instead of making decisions themselves. "I'll be here if you need help tearing down a barrier or getting around an obstacle," he assured me. But I was getting paid to command, and that's what he wanted me to do.

Fair enough. I can take a hint.

And I took Slattery at his word. I never once asked him to make a decision for me. But I also never asked permission either. Dusting off an old navy acronym UNODIR (unless otherwise directed), I kept him informed but never sought his consent. In fact, I might have gone a bit too far with it. I heard later, during one of the Middle East crises, that Slattery was complaining, "I wish Abrashoff would call or write and let me know what's going on." He himself was soon to be deployed to the Middle East, and to do his job well he needed briefings from me. A commodore has higher-ups he has to satisfy too.

I started touching base more often, providing biweekly situation reports, which seemed to strike a happy medium. As boss, he knew what was going on and could perform well enough to get his promotions. But I was still in full control of my job and wasn't asking him to do it for me. I have never told Commodore Slattery the effect he had on me just by uttering two simple words: take command.

The judicious use of UNODIR can actually create an environment where overall productivity and effectiveness improve—all because somebody was willing to risk going out on a limb. I did just that when I gave another commanding officer (a full-bird captain) in my battle group situation reports that identified his ship as the source of a computer problem that was dogging the entire group.

The problem involved what we call the link, an open chain of data that goes from ship to ship until everybody in the battle group is connected. Basically, the link was a way of joining *Benfold*'s two-hundred-mile radar range to the next ship's two-hundred-mile range, and the next, and so on, thus increasing our tactical capability. Although crucial to our operating efficiency, individually and collectively, the link was always problematic. That's because it requires millions of lines of computer code, and each vessel or shore station involved has its own electronic platform, which makes for an amazing variety of technology and software.

The system was supposedly interoperable, but in reality it was a mishmash. Compatibility problems were rampant. Quality would be great one day, awful the next. Then my crew started to notice that whenever one particular ship went off duty, the link improved. That ship's crew wasn't doing anything wrong; it was just an anomaly in the navy-provided computer program. But, clearly, there was something about the ship's platform that was troublesome.

Nothing in the rules encouraged me to do anything about the problem, especially since the offending ship's captain might have seen it as an embarrassment (which it wasn't). Nevertheless, instead of issuing a message to the entire battle group saying this ship was the source, I started sending private situation reports to him, quietly filling him in on what my crew and I had observed. I could have been cut off at the knees for challenging a captain about to become an admiral. Fortunately, the captain was a conscientious guy who recognized that I was only trying to help him do his job better, which would, in turn, allow the entire group to function better. He soon took it upon himself to publicly identify the problem his ship's transmissions were causing, which enabled the navy software programmers to focus on his software and fix the problem. He then linked through another ship, producing far better results for all the ships involved.

During his time in Iraq, Buddy Gengler learned a lot about UNODIR, but the issues involved were far more immediate and serious than a bad computer connection. When his team battled Saddam

Hussein loyalists, raided suspected insurgent sites, took prisoners, and fought their way out of ambushes, Buddy often found himself in situations where the rules dictated one set of actions and his brain (or heart) demanded another.

"The orders often said not to go into a particular area or not to take a particular kind of action," Buddy told me, "but as a quick-reaction force, we were there to get weapons off the street. If we realized there were weapons in the forbidden areas or buildings, then we went in. We just did. It could have gone wrong. We could have raided a building where the door was booby-trapped. But we went about it carefully and it worked out. We got the job done."

And isn't getting the job done what it's all about? Leaders take the initiative, and intelligent commanders and bosses recognize and reward such behavior, particularly when it succeeds. "When we got back from those missions, with the trucks full of weapons that nobody was going to use against American soldiers, everybody patted us on the back," Buddy said. "Few people will punish you for taking the initiative when you've got the right thing in your heart and mind." When the stakes are high, and the goal within reach, he added, it's better to ask for forgiveness than for permission.

Rules make perfect sense when they are written, but neither life nor business is static. They are dynamic and ever changing. The value we as leaders add is to interpret those rules—commander's intent, if you will—according to what is happening on the battlefield, and then adapt our actions to get the best results.

One of the army's rules of encounter is that the senior member of the team is never the first person to attack an enemy position. The object is to preserve the leadership on the ground. It's easy to understand the reasoning behind the rule; if the leader is down, the whole team, not to mention the mission, may be jeopardized. Buddy broke that rule when his heart told him he had to, but he was fully aware of the possible consequences and ready to accept them.

One night Buddy's team found itself outside an underground shelter where armed insurgents were thought to be holed up. The team could see that the bunker was a spacious, carpeted room, apparently constructed just before the war began, but the lights had been turned off. Buddy could hear people talking in the dark. He ordered his corporal to hold tight to a strap on Buddy's back so he could lean far into the space. A light on the end of his weapon would let him check out the situation and shoot quickly if he had to. But when he peeked in, Buddy could see that there was no need to shoot: The space sheltered a bunch of Iraqi civilians—men, women, and children who had gone underground in hopes of surviving the chaos that raged overhead.

When the team returned to base, the corporal approached the lieutenant. "Sir, you can't do that anymore," he said. "You're not supposed to go in first that way." Buddy merely remarked that the corporal had three kids. Buddy has no children.

"The rules are the rules," Buddy told me. "I know that. If there had been a guy sitting in that bunker with a weapon at the ready, I would have been dead meat. But I was willing to accept that as long as it meant that the corporal was going to go home to his kids."

All great leaders I know do not just blindly follow orders. They do their best to understand the commander's intent and apply it to each situation. That's where leaders provide value. To do anything different would mean we are nothing more than order takers, and order takers don't take ownership. They don't keep their people safe in a dog-eat-dog world. Just ask Buddy Gengler.

LESSON: Know when to pull rank, and when to forget it.

Buddy's his name, and a good buddy is what he is—but not to the men and women he commands. Buddy Gengler knows there's a line he can't cross: leaders shouldn't be buddies.

That's not much of a problem for some officers and business bosses I know. They're definitely of the old school, aloof, holding themselves above their people, issuing orders from on high. Nowadays, in the navy and in corporate ranks as well, there is a great emphasis on building a "relationship" with your team members. Just how close that connection should be, though, is up for grabs. I say not too close. Command Master Chief Bob Scheeler, who served with me on *Benfold*, helped me to understand why.

Like military life everywhere, the navy is governed by rank, seniority, and military discipline, and some officers really enjoy all that. They feel the need to stick out their chests full of medals and revel in the salutes and other formalities. I got my ego stroked by knowing that the sailors under my command were working on the best damn ship in the navy. Sometimes, though, my attitude frustrated Scheeler, and he let me know about it.

Scheeler was the spitting image of the salty seaman—a big tattooed guy from Laramie, Wyoming, with close-cropped hair and a mustache. And because of his rank as the senior enlisted officer, he represented the entire enlisted population to the captain and the executive officer, and he carried great weight on *Benfold*.

The command master chief, in his role as senior enlisted adviser, is an interesting navy invention, and every ship and submarine afloat has a command master. Scheeler was an engineman by trade, but the CMC could have come from any of several ratings—the gas turbine technician; the hull technician; the damage-control person, who helps put out fires and floods; the operations specialist; the electronic warfare specialist; and so on. It all depends on who wants the job—lots of guys don't want anything to do with it because it requires more than just technical skills. Command Master Chief Scheeler, for instance, had to worry about the whole ship, not just the diesel engines that he knew like the back of his hand.

The CMC's duties are not completely defined and can be molded according to the needs of the CO and XO. But any commanding officer who doesn't make full use of the command master chief's talents will never have a great ship. By the same token, you will never see a good ship that doesn't have a great command master chief. *Benfold* wasn't just a good ship, it was a great ship; and Master Chief Scheeler deserved a huge share of the credit. He spent his entire career busting a gut.

One day Scheeler came to protest my order that people shouldn't snap to attention every time I came into a room. I had been embarrassed by it and thought the constant work stoppages whenever I happened to stroll by were a complete waste of time and taxpayer dollars. Scheeler thought otherwise. He told me I was compromising the ship's discipline. He feared the sailors would begin to take me for granted and lose respect for my authority.

Because I valued Scheeler's experience and judgment, I followed his advice—and, in hindsight, I'm glad I did. I still don't like all the pomp and circumstance, but I understand that a leader has to maintain a certain stature to get his shipmates to buy into his cause.

By definition, leaders have to tell their teams what to do. Whether you reach decisions by intuition, straightforward logic, or consensus, at the end of the day you must still give the orders. If those orders are to be readily obeyed, your team members must have a healthy respect for the authority of the order giver. That means that you have to be separate from them, to a greater or lesser degree, and more than equal. If that respectful distance is breached, you will have a hard time leading— as Buddy Gengler discovered shortly after he was assigned to lead the rocket-launch platoon and found his new soldiers wanting.

An efficient radio operation is critical to ensure the accurate two-way transmission of orders from above and information from below. It didn't take long for Buddy to spot serious trouble. On more than one occasion, as he monitored the flow of messages from battalion headquarters into the rocket-launch radio room, Buddy heard a mangled version delivered to the commander. When Buddy investigated, he discovered soldiers on radio duty reading magazines, listening to music on their own headphones, and generally goofing off.

Come to find out, Buddy's new platoon had a terrible reputation within the battalion as being sloppily run and inefficient. Among other things, many of its soldiers were in poor physical shape. Searching for the cause led Buddy directly to the platoon sergeant. The sergeant had become so close to the men and women under his command, so much one of the guys, that he had lost their respect as a leader.

Arm wrestling, playing cards, joking around—"It ruined his credibility among the soldiers," Buddy said. "They did not respect him because the line was not there between I'm your boss and I'm your friend." When a soldier messed up, fell asleep on guard duty, or otherwise misbehaved, the sergeant would let it slide. He never came down hard on his people when they needed it. Predictably, they relaxed, did as little as possible, and lost all sense of pride in themselves and their unit. The soldiers actually told Buddy, "We need a leader who will hold us accountable."

The sergeant was upset when Buddy laid it all out for him. He saw himself as a benign and compassionate leader, a true friend to his soldiers. "The problem is, that just doesn't work," Buddy says. "Taking care of soldiers in combat means seeing to it that their weapons are cleaned, they are awake, they are sharp. It's not holding hands and singing 'Kumbaya.' You have to hold them accountable."

The same goes for people in your business or organization. They probably won't need someone to see to it that their weapons are cleaned, but most of us sometimes need a little prodding to do what needs doing. And all of us need "orders" if we are to serve the enterprise effectively. If you don't act like the captain of the ship and keep a strong hand on the wheel, you can expect your business to drift aimlessly.

The platoon sergeant was moved to a new assignment, replaced by someone who shared Buddy's leadership philosophy. Each soldier was then told what was expected of him or her, and those who didn't meet expectations were called on the carpet. A soldier who fell asleep on duty, for instance, ended up getting what's called an Article 15 (placed on report), which can end in punishment and even court-martial if the offense is serious enough. This particular soldier came close to losing his stripes.

"Everybody's eyes popped open," Buddy said. "They finally realized we meant business. It turned the whole platoon around, and soon we had as good or better a reputation as any unit in the battalion."

All of which is not to say that you cannot ever join your troops for a social event. There are times when it makes sense to ignore rank. The trick is to find the right occasion, and to keep those occasions to a minimum.

Buddy used the battery softball team to interact informally with his soldiers. On the ball field, people tend to forget about rank, he said. Everybody razzes each other; they're just there to have a good time. Buddy's team, drawn from a battery of just 110 soldiers, played against teams from units four times that size and won the division tournament. "That was really huge," Buddy said, and grinned.

Afterward he threw a big party where rank was forgotten, and where his unit came together in ways that proved invaluable after they were deployed to Iraq. "Having those moments where you break down the formal lines and really capture who another person is when he's not in uniform just deepens a relationship that you already have at the workplace," Buddy explained. Those bonds helped ease the stress of pressure-cooker days in the Middle East.

But even as he talked about the comradeship of the party—the kidding around, arms thrown over shoulders, the letting down of barriers—Buddy pointedly added: "I was one of the boys for a night. The next day, though, we went back to work, and the line between me and them was back in place. They knew that line. They knew it perfectly."

An organization is weakened when leaders become too buddy-buddy with those they lead. Your people must never forget who's boss. Otherwise, discipline breaks down and your troops may question your judgment and balk at following your command when you give an order to do something they don't want to do. In the military, insubordination puts the survival of your troops at risk.

On *Benfold*, I never socialized with the crew aside from joining activities like a shipwide outing to a baseball game or our Thursday night jazz or cookout on the flight deck. I needed to keep some distance between us. The biggest challenge in this regard arises when you are promoted from within the ranks and suddenly become your teammates' leader. Where, previously, you were all just buds, now you're in charge. How do you handle that kind of situation? If you socialized and went out with them before, I don't think you necessarily need to stop it altogether. But both you and they need to understand who is the boss, so when you have to make a decision, they will support you without question.

It's also crucial that you not play favorites. If you had one or two particular friends that you palled around with before, and now you're in charge of, say, twenty people, it sends a bad message if you continue to pal around with only the one or two. Everyone else starts wondering if you're playing favorites.

After I left *Benfold*, I worked mostly with civilians. Every evening one of the higher-ups would go to happy hour with two or three of his workers. And, granted, these people were outgoing and a lot of fun to be with. But it gave the perception to the other civilians that these chosen few had the inside track when it came time for promotions and would be treated differently than everyone else. Even I, rightly or wrongly, assumed as much.

So if you're going to go out to happy hour after work or socialize in other ways with those you lead, you need to invite everyone and make sure they know they are truly welcome. Any suspicion of favoritism will completely destroy morale and effectiveness.

Buddy Gengler figured that out. Sure, you can play baseball with your troops or go out for a beer as long as everyone is invited to join in. But if you only spend time with one or two or three favorites, you risk alienating everyone else. You must be ultrasensitive to what those who are left out will think. One of our great challenges as leaders is to show no favoritism and make sure that everyone has an equal shot.

LESSON: Stand up for your troops.

In my experience, nothing so binds your team members to you, nothing so strengthens their commitment to your cause, as your willingness to go to bat for them—even when you know you probably can't win. The time and energy you spend helping your people is an investment that never stops yielding dividends.

While Buddy was in Iraq, a member of his platoon came to him with a problem. He had just heard via the Red Cross that a loved one was seriously ill, and he wanted permission to go home. Buddy remembers that the relationship, while a very close one, definitely did not meet the immediate-family criteria for compassionate leave from a war zone.

The soldier was understandably upset. He pointed out that the platoon was near the end of its tour and about to be shipped back home anyway. He explained to Buddy how the person's illness was affecting his children. Buddy decided he had to give it his best shot, even though it was no small project.

To begin with, Buddy gathered reports from the soldier's immediate superior that showed his outstanding record, and copied text describing awards the soldier had received. He composed a long memorandum listing the soldier's compassionate, self-sacrificing, and self-motivating qualities as well as his achievements.

When the file was complete, Buddy called the soldier into his office and asked him to read it. "I told him I couldn't guarantee that it would work, but I intended to send the file to the commanding officer and I was going to do everything I could to get him back with his family. The tears welled in his eyes. He couldn't believe someone would take the time and effort to put all this stuff together."

As Buddy had feared, the appeal was denied. Ironically, a major reason for the rejection was the unit's upcoming departure for home. Because the soldier was a maintenance specialist, he would be needed to repair the vehicles when the unit moved out. But the CO did allow the soldier extended phone privileges, which he used to try to console his wife for his continued absence.

That episode formed a special bond between Buddy and the soldier. "Anything I needed," said Buddy, "he did it, and did it over and beyond the standard. He exceeded standards in everything he did. I really think that's a direct result of my taking the time and proving that I was willing to go the extra mile for him."

Interesting, isn't it, how going to bat for the guy ended up making him a better soldier. That was not, however, Buddy's motivation. "I did it because I care about every one of my soldiers, and it was the right thing to do."

LESSON: Ask your crew what's wrong with the ship.

If you have no real sense of what your team members are thinking, you will have a hard time getting them on board your cause. You may want to motivate them to work harder and better, but how can you know where to start if you're ignorant about their feelings toward you, their jobs, and the larger organization? They are not going to take responsibility for their jobs, for example, if you never address their grievances— or, for that matter, never even bother to find out what the grievances are. Of course, once you find out where your people are coming from, you have to go there and try to fix things. Asking for answers but then failing to respond to them makes a mockery of leadership.

When Buddy was given command of the rocket-launch platoon in Fort Hood, Texas, he surveyed each of his new teammates on four topics:

- List three good things about the platoon.
- List three bad things.
- What are three things that would improve your morale?
- What are your goals in life?

After the surveys came back, Buddy spent fifteen to twenty minutes with each soldier discussing his responses. He found the results dumbfounding.

To start with, the soldiers were unhappy that their leaders weren't holding them more accountable by setting a standard of performance and forcing them to meet it. Their platoon was being ridiculed because of its sloppy vehicle maintenance, low scores on physical training tests, and losing sports teams—and they were embarrassed by that.

"In the army," Buddy said, "there's a lot of crap talk about whether you're a good or bad platoon and who beats whom in sports. My guys wanted to do better in every way."

There were other surprises. The soldiers wanted a chess tournament, and they wanted to get college credits. Buddy listened hard—and then responded.

First off, he made accountability a priority. Every performance indicator in the platoon—from vehicle maintenance to physical training to clean sleeping areas to guard alertness—was identified and scored each month. In short order, the platoon's failure rate improved to 25 percent from 75 percent.

Next, Buddy set up a chess tournament and offered a forty-minute phone call home as the prize. He also organized tournaments in checkers, spades, and touch football. "It was all a lot of fun for the guys," Buddy remembered, "and their morale and their pride in themselves and the platoon really jumped."

Meanwhile, those soldiers who wanted to pursue college credits were instructed on how to do it long distance—and how to get the army to pay for it. "They didn't even know it was an option," Buddy said.

In the end, a so-so platoon was transformed into a top-notch do-it-better outfit committed to a common goal of excellence—all because its leader had the good sense to ask his troops what they wanted.

LESSON: Show the way by your own actions.

Here's how my dictionary defines the verb *lead:* "To show the way to others, usually by going ahead of them." Nothing so impresses followers as the sight of their leader out there on point, living up to the performance standards he has laid down for them. Leaders who sit at desks, with their doors shut, and push paper around don't fit the definition. They are not going to inspire their people to give their all for the team.

Buddy offered a dramatic example of the kind of loyalty you can inspire when you lead the way. Heading up a mission to clear out a suspected insurgent's house in Iraq, he and a group from his platoon were transported to the site in a Bradley armored vehicle. When they stormed out of the Bradley, they immediately realized they were too far from the house they wanted to attack.

Buddy started running, his men following. Like the rest of them, he was wearing a heavy vest and carrying ammunition and his weapon. When he got to the house, however, he turned to see his men very slowly bringing up the rear—they were still sixty or so yards behind him. For several seconds until his men caught up, Buddy was alone and exposed.

The mission itself was a success, but that night he called his troops together and read them the riot act. "You almost cost me my life today," he told them. But he said he knew they bore him no malice; the problem was that "you didn't have the wind or the physical ability to keep up to save me." Their eyes got wide, Buddy said, "Like: 'Oh, they always told us to be in shape, but they didn't tell us why. Now we know why.'"

Although physical training was a required activity, the platoon hadn't taken it seriously—except for Buddy, who was in excellent physical condition. Before they shipped out from the United States, Buddy said, they ate as if "every night was the last supper." For the next few weeks, as they waited to get into Iraq, they floated on ships in the Mediterranean and put on even more pounds. Once they were in combat, they came back to base hot and exhausted. It was all too easy to put off physical training.

But after Buddy's close call, PT classes were convened every morning. "It was hot as hell, even in the morning," he said, "but they showed up, even the guys who were going on patrol that day." Before long, Buddy's soldiers had lost a tremendous amount of weight and greatly improved their stamina.

Buddy could have lectured his team about the importance of physical training until he was blue in the face, and he still might never have persuaded them to sign on and get in shape. But because his fitness contrasted so sharply with their own poor physical condition—and because they were shocked that they had actually put Buddy in harm's way—his strong example both energized the team and constantly reinforced the positive rewards to be gained from meeting the performance standards.

IT'S BEEN MY HONOR AND PLEASURE OVER THE YEARS TO serve with many young men like First Lieutenant Buddy Gengler. The U.S. military has always attracted the best this country has to offer. Smart, savvy, full of love and pride for their country, and dedicated to their jobs, these young people possess leadership skills that are extraordinary. Most, like Buddy, do their jobs every day with few complaints and little recognition outside their immediate spheres of influence. They have a lot to teach us about being the kind of leaders who can excite a band of brothers and sisters to follow us anywhere.

LESSONS

Call in the reserves when you need them.
Dare your crew to be the best,
and they will deliver.
Don't rush to judgment.
Learn from your bad experiences.
Know when to ignore the rules,
and be prepared to take the heat.
Know when to pull rank, and when to forget it.
Stand up for your troops.
Ask your crew what's wrong with the ship.
Show the way by your own actions.

CHAPTER 2

CEO Trish Karter Makes the Deer Dance

*Sure, great flavor means good money. But the sweetest success
for this thriving bakery derives from its working conditions—
an ambience that feeds the staff's appetite for good food,
good taste, and good fun.*

ANY HUMAN ENTERPRISE WORKS BEST IF IT'S INSPIRED BY A
sense of mission. When I was in the U.S. Navy, it was common
enough to see officers and enlisted people alike merely serving time,
staying out of trouble, and hoping to retire with a nice military pension. But I wanted my crew to buy into my cause of making USS *Benfold* the best damn ship in the navy. In two short years we lived up to
that promise because we were dedicated to something besides collecting a paycheck. And that holds true in business too. Sure, making
money is necessary and wonderful, but it is not the real reward. Money
is the yardstick for measuring success; dedication, enthusiasm, and joy
are the rewards.

By any reckoning, the Dancing Deer Baking Company is a flour-
ishing success story. Just ten years old, the bakery, based in Roxbury,
Massachusetts, an inner-city district of Boston, has built a thriving
market for its high-end cakes and cookies in outlets serving gourmets
across the nation. Revenues at the privately held company reached five
million dollars in its 2004 fiscal year and were expected to soar well beyond that mark in fiscal 2005, partly because Dancing Deer's growing

online business has won rave reviews from all sorts of national media, including NBC's *Today* show.

Dancing Deer is the creation of a diverse trio of talented people: Suzanne Lombardi, an expert baker who originated many of its enduring recipes; Ayis Antoniou, a physicist, business strategist, and devoted amateur cook; and Trish Karter, an artist, businessperson, and passionate environmentalist. Suzanne and Ayis have moved on to pursue other interests, while Trish, who was once married to Ayis, has ended up running the company and turning herself into a masterful leader.

Dancing Deer was conceived in 1994 as a way to ride the then new gourmet coffee wave by supplying delectable, all-natural baked goods for dunkers at restaurants and café chains like Starbucks. Originally headquartered in a former pizza parlor on a busy corner in Boston's inner-city Roxbury district, Dancing Deer now occupies a remodeled, turn-of-the-century brewery at 77 Shirley Street.

Soon after Dancing Deer introduced its line of packaged goods in 1996, its baking crew filled the street with aromas so tantalizing that passersby demanded access. Suddenly, the founders had a retail as well as a wholesale business, both exuding the sweet smell of success. In fact, just two years later Dancing Deer's irresistible molasses clove cookie captured the top prize at the National Association of Specialty Food Trade convention—the food industry's equivalent of a Hollywood Oscar. More than a baker's dozen of product awards and business honors have followed in the intervening years, including six additional "Oscars" for mouthwatering treats like Dancing Deer's deep dark gingerbread and chocolate espresso cakes and its chocolate tangerine and sugar cane lime cookies. Powered by the public recognition (Dancing Deer gives new meaning to word-of-mouth advertising), the company's mail-order and online businesses first set sail in 1999 and haven't slowed since. Along the way, Dancing Deer has regularly channeled significant dollars into philanthropy, notably through its Sweet Home Project for, among other things, helping homeless people in Roxbury.

All of which goes to prove that even in megachain America, it's still possible for an offbeat upstart like Dancing Deer to succeed with old-fashioned purity. Its line of perishable goodies are baked from scratch, using all natural ingredients without artificial preservatives, and packaged artfully with what the company calls "a whimsical disregard for the expected."

But products and packaging alone don't add up to business success. If that were the case, I could have slapped a much-needed coat of paint on *Benfold*, cruised to victory in a competition or two, and called it a career. No, a winning organization is built on leadership—and not just at the top, but throughout the organization. Trish Karter understands this completely. She also understands that leadership means bringing people together in a common cause. From the beginning, Dancing Deer Bakery has been about people joining hands and hearts to achieve a short list of shared goals.

No one comes to Dancing Deer without a love of food in general and bakery delights in particular. Running a close second is the crew's passionate commitment to a job well done, which means there's no such thing as a nine-to-five day in this fast-growth company. As I will describe in greater detail a few pages ahead, another prerequisite for Dancing Deer recruits, and one that I heartily endorse, is a willingness to communicate. Passive-aggressive personalities need not apply. "Deers," as they style themselves, must talk, share ideas, even endure a bit of conflict because that's what it takes to create and perpetuate excellence.

With these attributes as the raw ingredients, Dancing Deer has, in very short order, achieved all of its growth and profit goals. Perhaps more important, this potent mix has also enabled the company to fulfill its founders' fondest dream of building something that transcends mere business, an enterprise that weighs its achievement on a broader scale than profits made or lost. Nonprofit organizations appreciate the rewards that come from pursuing a greater goal, of course, and so do ex-military men like me. But for many an organization, the success of a company such as Dancing Deer may provide a wake-up call long overdue.

Trish claims she has no fixed recipe for success. But there's one essential ingredient—more important even than flour and sugar—and that's leadership. Among the lessons she's learned:

LESSON: Success transcends the bottom line.

From the start, Dancing Deer epitomized the notion that there's more to life than making money. Suzanne Lombardi, the baker whose recipes and entrepreneurial energy provided the life spark, was determined to create exceptional baked goods using only natural ingredients, environmentally sound methods, and recyclable packaging, all enhanced by ethical marketing standards and her insistence that the business should be fun. Although Suzanne left the bakery in 2000 to start an organic candy company, the original principles, which Trish has adopted as her own, still animate Dancing Deer. (Another of Suzanne's legacies is the bakery's name. It was borrowed from her grandmother's antique store in Bar Harbor, Maine, while the inspiration for Dancing Deer's best-selling deep dark gingerbread cake came from her grandmother's recipe box.)

"We hold really tight to our values," Trish told me. It is Trish's artistic sense and direction that is behind the look of Dancing Deer's packaging and Web site, and as noted, it was Trish's business acumen that helped Suzanne turn her baking hobby into a going concern. Trish, who met Suzanne when she was just starting out, persuaded her husband Ayis Antoniou, a physicist and business consultant with a passion for food, to back the venture. And when business success began to overwhelm Suzanne, Trish volunteered to introduce structure and systems to bring order to the Dancing Deer operation.

The company nearly collapsed, however, when Trish's marriage began to fall apart. The struggle to keep Dancing Deer alive drained her emotionally, Trish told me, and convinced her of the importance of Dancing Deer being "something more than just a way to make a living."

Natural food principles and a concern for the environment still rule at Dancing Deer, and ownership is baked into the cake from the bottom layer up. Trish takes pride in hiring and training a culturally diverse group of workers from surrounding Roxbury and other Boston neighborhoods, helping them learn English, and giving them opportunities to grow and advance. Every permanent employee has shares or options in the business. And, as previously mentioned, Dancing Deer is also committed to returning a significant part of its earnings to the community. For example, it is a major financial supporter of One Family, a coalition of nonprofit organizations dedicated to ending homelessness. The group helps families attain economically stable lives and homes of their own through a variety of direct action programs. Thirty-five percent of the retail sales of Dancing Deer's Sweet Home line of products goes to support the homelessness project. "We help people happily," Trish explained. "I want Dancing Deer to be a model of how positive a force small business can be."

And, indeed, that is one reason why I wanted to feature Trish Karter in this book. Small businesses have become the engine of job growth in this country, but small-business owners don't always have the time or money to invest in the tools that can help get them to the next level of leadership.

As you can see, Dancing Deer truly is as much a cause as it is a corporation, and its success supports the notion that products get better in proportion to how much workers love what they do. Authoritarian leaders who instill fear rather than love will strenuously object. But when it comes to the Dancing Deer Baking Company, the proof is so real you can literally taste it.

There are no mandates governing business that say Dancing Deer must support its Roxbury community. Trish Karter and her company do it simply because it's the right thing to do. Every worthwhile enterprise—and that includes the U.S. Navy—accepts some responsibility for lessening the total sum of misery in the world.

The navy does it, in part, through Project Handclasp, a program established in 1962 to foster mutual understanding, respect, and goodwill between U.S. sailors and people of other nations. Based in my longtime home port of San Diego, Project Handclasp accepts donations from businesses, individuals, and religious and service organizations—everything from toys to tools—and Navy ships deliver them to the impoverished around the world.

When we knew *Benfold* was setting sail for a particular port, we contacted Project Handclasp to see if it had any donated items we could take along. I recognized that what we were doing was, pure and simple, the right thing to do, but I was also mindful that as a leader, I should set an example for my crew. I not only expected them to be skilled at their jobs and tough enough to withstand anything an enemy might throw at us, but I also wanted them to recognize that there were other standards by which a crew and its commander could be judged. Compassion counted.

So when we visited Puerto Vallarta on Mexico's west coast, we delivered Project Handclasp sewing machines and toys to an orphanage. But that was just the beginning. In Puerto Vallarta, just as in every other place to which we delivered donated materials and equipment, the sailors quickly surveyed the situation. What they saw was a rundown institution in a desperately poor area with nothing like what it needed to care for its young charges. So my sailors set to work with paintbrushes, saws, and hammers, spending hours of their own time improving the place.

Aside from buying a little paint or other materials, I had nothing to do with this part of the visits. The sailors themselves organized the work crews, enlisting probably 20 percent of the whole crew in the cause. Because so many of my sailors had never been handed much of anything in their own young lives, they seemed particularly attuned to the need for help in these impoverished areas.

On the Puerto Vallarta trip, Seaman Attila Yilmaz was, as usual, one of the organizers. A smart guy and a talented technician who kept our electronic warfare equipment in superb order, Attila had spent his early years in foster homes. He knew what it meant to be poor and without family. He could easily have grown into a mean-spirited and stingy man, but he didn't. Instead, he was compassionate—and a leader in the making.

Most people don't know that community support is, in fact, into the fabric of the entire U.S. military; soldiers and sailors give generously to the United Way. On *Benfold,* we held raffles and other fund-raising events to give back to the larger community through the United Way, or to our own service community through the Navy-Marine Corps Relief Society. I never took notes on which sailors were donating and which weren't, and no promotion points were awarded, yet these young men and women, who don't make much in the first place, annually collected fifteen thousand dollars for the United Way and about twenty thousand dollars for the relief society, which provides emergency loans and grants to sailors, marines, and their families. Say you're deployed on a destroyer like *Benfold* and your wife is at home and her car breaks down. She needs the car to get to work, but there's no cash readily available for repairs. The relief society will offer a loan to tide her over.

If you need more proof of the generosity of our young U.S. soldiers, look no further than Iraq, where many sacrifice their free time to get schools up and running again or to work on other community projects in the towns where they are based. Engaged in the dangerous and often thankless job of trying to keep the peace, they will gladly tell you how much they enjoy the chance to interact with Iraqis in a positive way. They hope their community service will help to change negative attitudes about the United States and its troops.

That is just one example of how doing good can also bring tangible rewards. Building goodwill in a local community always benefits any kind of organization. It makes sense for the U.S. military to develop friends on the ground because it's better to leaven the fear engendered by our technical might with a healthy dose of respect for our attitudes and values. By the same token, it makes good business sense for a company to give back to the community not just because it's the right thing to do, but because it creates a positive environment in which to operate. And when a company invests in local educational projects, for example, the benefits are direct and tangible in the form of a better-educated local workforce.

Successful leaders like Trish Karter know for a fact that achievement is not measured in promotions or profitability alone. The investment of the heart is just as important as the investment of the head.

LESSON: Don't become a bottleneck.

Trish Karter's introduction to business wasn't easy. Halfway through her senior year as an art history major at Wheaton College, she left school to help her father steer his faltering industrial-scale recycling venture through a Chapter 11 reorganization.

"The father of modern-day bottle and can recycling," Trish called him, the master of his ship and his daughter's hero. Peter Karter, who founded Branford, Connecticut-based Resource Recovery Systems, understood that most people would never conscientiously do the chore of cleaning used cans and bottles and separating glass by color, so he invented reliable technology that would do the job. His process turned out streams of glass shards so clean and consistent that they could go straight into a bottle maker's melting vats. "The whole family had been very much involved in the business and the cause," Trish explained, and when it foundered, "I jumped in as a young, idealistic college kid. It turned out I learned a lot about cash flow and equipment, investors and marketing. I've been in that world one way or another ever since."

Trish's first lesson in business was the importance of making a payroll. She sometimes helped shovel glass into a delivery truck to top off the load, rode the truck to the buyer's scale, took the receipt to the buyer's office and collected the check, then raced to the bank to deposit it in time to cover the next day's payroll. Anyone who's ever sweated making the payroll knows the anxiety involved.

But Trish's most important lesson dealt with leadership. She described her father, the son of poor Greek immigrants, as "a charismatic leader, an optimist, and passionately dedicated to his cause." Sensing his depth of commitment and strong belief in what he was doing—the marks of a true leader—others were willing to give him their money, time, and effort. "There's no substitute for that kind of leadership by heroic effort," she told me. But that alone isn't enough, she added: "You can't really run at that pace over the long haul."

Trish applied those insights in 2003 when she found herself drained and exhausted from carrying too much of the Dancing Deer load. "The company was growing, and we were doing well," she recalled, but "at the pace I was going, with all I had on my plate, I didn't feel I could take it to the next level. Sometimes I just couldn't process everything fast enough. I was in too many places. I was holding us back." So she took a hard look at what her real talents were and gradually began replacing herself "in anything I don't think I'm really good at. I've been restructuring the organization so that I have successfully removed myself as a bottleneck."

Recognizing that she couldn't do it all led Trish to recruit a marketing director to take over two of Dancing Deer's sales channels. For a position so critical to the company's continued success, Trish wanted to search far and wide, so she broadcast her request for candidates through her e-mail network. She was flooded with résumés. Trish spoke directly to almost every candidate, fearful of somehow overlooking the perfect choice. "I kissed a lot of frogs," she quipped. But when the prince finally arrived, Trish knew it within forty-five minutes.

The decision to divide up some of Trish's duties has made the company stronger. "I was too critical to too many pieces of the organization," Trish reflected, "and I'm not anymore." For someone with more ego and less self-confidence, saying that "people don't miss me" could be devastating, but Trish recognizes that having talented associates who can step in and do what she once did is good for the company—and good for her personally too. "I could disappear for weeks, and it really wouldn't make any big difference to the day-to-day operations in the company," she said with more relief than regret.

Trish's story reminds me of the situation I found on USS *England,* where my commanding officer presided over two horrendous bottlenecks—one incoming, one outgoing.

When I came aboard, the ship was in the process of being certified for deployment to the Middle East. I was the tactical action officer stationed in the combat information center, which had numerous radios and headsets scattered about the room. Because *England* was a multimission ship, each radio was keyed to a different circuit to receive calls from the air defense coordinator, the antisurface-ship warfare commander, and the antisubmarine warfare coordinator. During certification, the calls were coming fast and furious over all radios. The problem was that no one was answering them. Why? Because ship policy designated only a few select officers to handle the radios. On that particular day just one person in the room was permitted to answer the calls—me.

I rushed from one phone to another, taking a call from the commander of the battle group, receiving another with directions on how to maneuver our ship, and another with orders to attack a simulated target. The members of the watch team just stood there while I zipped around like the Road Runner cartoon character, all in a sweat and unable to attend to my real job of directing their actions based on the messages being received. I was too busy taking calls to tell anyone anything. Common sense told me the watch team should be on the phones, relaying messages to me. I looked really, really stupid.

When it came to any correspondence leaving *England,* the captain was a real stickler. He not only corrected grammar, he also recast phrases and entire sentences—not to alter the content but to improve its cadence. If you wrote *glad,* he would change it to *happy.* Talk about a bottleneck! Officers could spend hours every day waiting to get a message out while the captain did his editing. What made it worse was his insistence on explaining to the writer just why he had made all his changes. We didn't care at that point. We just wanted to go home. He had to work until eight o'clock every night because three hours of every afternoon got wasted this way.

When I took command of *Benfold,* I vowed never to be a bottleneck. I wanted every communication from the ship to be correct, of course, but if someone succeeded in getting the point across, I didn't do a rewrite just to fit my own style. I made a conscious decision:

rather than have my officers waste all those extra hours striving for perfection in the area of written communications, I'd be both happy and glad if my officers were freed to spend more time on our true bottom line—combat readiness.

LESSON: Bake teamwork into every cake.

If you are constantly setting up teams to handle new projects, you are not doing things the Dancing Deer way. "The whole concept here is that we *are* a team," Trish explained. "It is the way we think; it's built into everything we do."

Deers have individual roles and responsibilities, but no one is territorial about it. They take it for granted that everyone will chip in to handle a new challenge or a looming crisis. At the peak holiday season, for instance, when the company whips up 25 percent of its annual volume in just three weeks, there are "occasional needs for heroism," Trish said. "Everybody down to the packing room!" could be the lyric of a Dancing Deer holiday tune. At the call, anyone who can drops everything to pack sweet treats into holiday boxes.

Consequently, someone arriving at Dancing Deer with a nine-to-five, not-my-problem mentality won't stay long. Anyone who rejects the notion of shared responsibility "doesn't fit in with the culture of the place," Trish said. "I'll hear it from the organization that this person isn't a fit."

In its early days Dancing Deer typically hired bright, young, enthusiastic people who wanted to learn and weren't expecting to be paid anywhere near the top of the market. "As we've grown," Trish said, "we've grown salaries and everybody has done very well." On top of the rising wages, all permanent employees receive an actual ownership stake in the company, and every employee at every level receives stock options.

Monetary rewards are only a part of what motivates teamwork, however. On *Benfold*, where I had no control over how much the crew was paid, the intangible rewards of being a team were at least as coveted and important. So, too, at Dancing Deer, which looks for people who "want to be part of an enterprise they believe in," Trish said. "They want forward movement, opportunity, fun, excitement. They want to be able to be proud of who they are, what they do, and what the company stands for."

Teamwork also embraces the attitude that no work is unimportant, and no one is too important to do whatever needs to be done. Trish herself often pitches in on the brownie line in the seasonal rush, and Lissa McBurney, on her first week on the job as production manager, filled in for an ailing cookie supervisor. Lissa impressed her tough, hardworking Colombian and Salvadoran bakers by picking up sixty-pound tubs of molasses and slinging fifty-pound sacks of flour with the best of them. After that, no one questioned the authority of this thirtyish former fund-raiser who arrived at Dancing Deer by dint of a fascination with the food industry honed during the years she herself spent learning the basics as a professional baker. Lissa was accepted as the new boss, somebody who had paid her dues and could operate a cookie assembly line—and, yes, command respect.

Lissa is in charge of more than half the company in terms of number of employees, but she is only one of a five-member executive team that reports to Trish. Lissa's domain is downstairs, in the bakery, while upstairs belongs to Trish and her sales, marketing, and finance team. No two women could be less alike. Trish speaks in a warm, almost confidential tone, while Lissa is blunt, crisp, to the point. Trish's seemingly endless patience and openness to new ideas contrasts with Lissa's pragmatic, no-nonsense, and, as she herself puts it, "not at all conflict averse" demeanor.

What binds these two women and the rest of the team together in a shared effort is the well-being of the entire Dancing Deer crew. Trish hires great people, then works to fashion a job that fits their talents. Lissa gets to know them as individuals and fiercely protects their livelihoods. In an industry where part-time work is the norm and shortened hours or even layoffs are a necessary evil, they do what they can to provide job security. Permanent staffers know they can count on putting in their normal hours, even though they may have to scrub floors to fill the time. But everyone knows that on a team no work is unimportant. The attitude is: "Hey, here's the floor; we can scrub it every day until it shines," said Lissa.

In return for this loyalty, people rise to the occasion whenever needed. They put in extra time when business is extra good. They pitch in willingly on major projects such as the effort to make the bakery kosher friendly. And they take personal responsibility when problems surface and need solutions.

To me, the real question of leadership is this: Is your workforce battle ready? Can it get the job done when the chips are down? Dancing Deer can answer a resounding "Yes, sir!" Of course there's also a preliminary question for management: Have you done what it takes to develop a workforce that will do battle on your behalf? Here Trish and Lissa can shout out their own affirmation. And as you will discover momentarily, their workforce repays them with an all-battle-stations-ready response to trouble.

LESSON: Always be ready for surprise inspections.

In the navy we get inspected to death. There are so many certifications that it's hard to keep count. The galleys were inspected, as were my pay and personnel records. I had a post office on the ship, so people came and inspected the number of stamps I had on hand because I was required to have so many one-cent, two-cent, three-cent, and thirty-seven-cent stamps. Our sick bay got inspected to make sure we were providing proper health care to our sailors. We even got evaluated on the number of cavities the crew had. So here I was, a commanding officer charged with keeping a billion-dollar destroyer combat ready at all times, and I also had to worry about whether my sailors were brushing and flossing and getting their teeth cleaned. Come to think of it, being a ship's captain may be the closest thing to motherhood a man can experience.

Too often on some ships, though, the attitude is, "Okay, we have to do things right so we can pass the inspection." But that reasoning is wrongheaded. One of the first things I learned in the navy is that inspections are serious business and passing them is important—and not just to buff up your résumé. Inspections are a true measure of how well the ship is run on a day-in, day-out basis, and whether it's ready for action. Some captains toil for months to get into shape for their annual inspections, but as I've said before, after the first one I wanted *Benfold* to be so sharp that it could get top marks any day the inspectors happened to show up—and we met the challenge.

Trish Karter learned it the hard way at the Dancing Deer Baking Company, but she got the message that inspections aren't about looking good for the inspectors. Rather, they're about being absolutely positive that on every single day you are able to give your customers the best and safest product human hands can create.

Baked goods pose few health risks, so bakeries aren't required to undergo as stringent a regimen of state and federal inspections as some other food businesses. But their larger customers often ask that the bakeries be inspected for safety and sanitation problems by knowledgeable third parties.

Dancing Deer had put off inspections for several years to deal with what it considered more pressing problems, like developing the brand and increasing revenues. The plant was clean and safe, Trish said, but the hundred-year-old building was showing the wear and tear of age and the bakery's rapid growth. Ceilings needed painting, a few cracks had opened in the concrete floor, and the rubber safety coating on travel ramps was worn away at the edges.

Furthermore, written policy and documentation were lacking in some areas. Pot washers were shown how to use a three-compartment sink to wash, rinse, and sanitize, but there was no training manual nor were there logs to verify that anyone had been trained. Employees were not allowed to wear sandals or jewelry in the plant, but there was inadequate written policy to back up the rule.

The inspectors showed up without warning on a day when Lissa was out sick. Trish showed them around and tried to answer questions that could have been better handled by Lissa because of her firsthand knowledge.

The visit turned into a thorough embarrassment that triggered a major two-and-a-half-month overhaul of the plant and its processes. "We had the choice to repair and move on," recalled Lissa, "or to really improve the facility. We saw this as an opportunity to improve."

At Trish's direction, Lissa and a newly hired facilities manager compiled a huge list of every problem in the plant and all the documentation that would be required to prove the highest level of compliance with health and safety regulations.

Then a team was assembled to correct every problem on the list. They held almost daily meetings and divided into subteams for the more complex tasks. They reminded each other repeatedly about the leak in the bathroom pipe or the certification that needed updating. Lissa gave Best Bird Dog awards to those who sniffed out new problems and designated those who fixed them as Best Mover and Shaker.

Once content to train new employees merely by shadowing their work, Dancing Deer became a stickler for structure: policy and procedure manuals were written, inspection logs were established and maintained, and new employees were given formal training sessions. The company even made up a good-manufacturing-practices dance in which workers would wave their hands in the air and lift their feet at the announcement of a surprise check for jewelry-free hands, proper footwear, and so on.

The team toured the plant every week to measure progress. They held mock recalls (shades of my mock power losses on *Benfold*), pretending that all gingerbread cookies made that day had to be recalled because of a food-safety violation. Trish and Lissa—all the Deers, in fact—knew the product was safe (not to mention mouth-wateringly delicious), but "we just had to prove it to everybody else," Lissa told me. "We had been embarrassed and we never wanted to be embarrassed like that again." Spoken like a true leader.

And just like the crew on *Benfold,* the Deers discovered they were doing more than passing an inspection. They were raising the bar of daily performance. "We're doing it as an everyday way of acting now," Lissa said. "We're documenting. We're teaching people who don't know English how to fill out inspection forms for the freezer temperature every day, and teaching them why it's important to fill out an inspection form." The new standard is 100 percent compliance, achieved by constant focus on crucial details. It's tedious at times but well worth the effort, Lissa said. "This is how you increase the level of your professionalism and effectiveness."

But Dancing Deer is about more than just compliance. This is a company where everyone now knows the whys and wherefores. They know, for example, that wearing watches in the plant is verboten because stray food particles caught under a watchband or any piece of jewelry can create sanitation problems. Then there's the possibility of cross-contamination. "There are terrible anecdotes in the food industry," Lissa said, "stories of hundreds of thousands of pounds of cocoa being recalled and destroyed, all because of a missing watch crystal" that might wind up in someone's throat. In her characteristic no-nonsense manner, Lissa made it clear that such sloppy behavior would not be tolerated at Dancing Deer.

Amid all the grumbling about inspections, it's easy to forget that standards have a tendency to slide if no one is checking—and that's neither the right way to do business nor the right way to run a navy. The person at the top has to set the standards and explain, as Lissa did, why it's so important to maintain them at all times.

I guarantee that if you're scrimping on enforcing day-to-day standards, it will show in your performance. If your crew members get the idea that you are loosening the standards or that there's room for negotiation, they will begin to take liberties. Our standards on *Benfold* were never open to negotiation, and yours shouldn't be either. Standards are the criteria by which you are judged, either within your industry or your marketplace. If you hold them up as unbending, people will live them each and every day, and pretty soon they will become part of the culture of the place, affecting everything else you do.

In 1985, I went to work for Rear Admiral Hugh Webster was the commander of the Seventh Fleet's Naval Surface Co Force in Subic Bay, the Philippines. In eighteen months, we must have visited seventy ships, and I could tell a lot about a ship's performance the minute I came on board. If it was dirty, it didn't stand a chance of being a good performer. Being clean and shipshape didn't assure greatness, but I knew that such a vessel would be an above-average performer.

Because I knew that you can never have a great ship or a great organization if you don't adhere to your standards each and every day, I used to walk around *Benfold* picking up bits of trash. The sailors who owned the spaces from which the captain was gathering up Coke cans and other litter were extremely embarrassed. I could have ordered someone else to go around picking up trash, of course, but I thought my doing it would have more of an impact—and it sure did. My sailors got the signal I was sending about what was important on *Benfold*.

And as Trish learned, it's far easier to meet high standards on your own terms than to get a poor grade on inspection and be forced to play catch-up under the watchful eye of an outside authority figure. It's worse still if failure to adhere to standards causes you to lose the trust of your chain of command or your customers. If you screw up in front of customers, it may be hard, if not impossible, to regain the warm and fuzzy feeling they once felt for you. But when you set high standards and do great things each and every day, like Trish and her crew at Dancing Deer, the inspectors can show up any day and you'll pass with flying colors.

When the revamp at Dancing Deer was complete and the inspectors returned, the bakery got the highest possible rating. Trish called all her employees into the conference room and introduced them to the inspectors. They had a small celebration—a rah-rah moment, Lissa called it—capped off with a pizza party.

Pizza sounds pretty good, but when *Benfold* aced its first annual inspection, I took the crew on a tour of liberty ports. They had earned it.

LESSON: Throw a lifeline to struggling crewmates.

Sometimes, Trish explained, good employees hit a bad patch, and you have to get their minds turned back in the right direction. "I only have one way of doing it," she told me. "I dig in, and I spend time with that person."

Trish reminds me of a baseball coach. Anyone who follows the sport has suffered along with a favorite player who goes into a batting slump or just can't seem to throw strikes anymore. More often than not, it's a mental lapse that knocks ball players off stride, and a good coach will try to "talk" a player back to a higher performance level.

Trish, who acknowledged that she has managerial weaknesses, was passionate when she told me, "I care deeply about the people who work here, and everybody knows that." I tried to spread the same message among the *Benfold* crew, and I did it the same way—by sitting down with individual crew members and getting to know as much as I could about each one. It turned out to be some of the best time I spent in the navy, and it paid off hugely in morale and team spirit.

Trish's talks, which can last for hours, are therapylike sessions exploring an employee's problems, sorting out misunderstandings, setting goals, and renewing commitments to the job. She won't gloss over mistakes. However, she recognizes human frailty and thinks people usually respond well when she says something along the lines of: "That wasn't so smart, and you should have known better, but let's fix the damage and move forward, having learned from it."

Two interlaced people problems at Dancing Deer show how well Trish's approach works. In the first situation, Lissa was dealing with a cookie-line supervisor—let's call him Rob—who cultivated the image of a tough guy. With his shaved head, many body piercings, and visible tattoos, he was the very picture of a rebel. To make matters worse, Rob also had something of a short fuse.

Lissa went out of her way to keep Rob at Dancing Deer. Once, in a snit, he threatened to quit, but she wouldn't take the bait. Instead, she countered his impulsiveness with reasoned calm, saying: "All right, let's talk about why you want to do that." Their relationship smoothed out a bit after that, and Rob lost his defensiveness. In time, he proved himself a talented manager who could solve problems and inspire loyalty in his staff. The attitude adjustment eventually earned Rob a promotion to bakery manager, a new position that made him responsible for all the bakers—of cakes as well as cookies.

Not everyone was pleased, however. His advancement came as a blow to the cake supervisor Milton, another longtime employee who had heaved pallets around in the packing room when he first arrived, fresh from El Salvador. Milton was a clean-cut Latino of great faith and respect for authority, and he worked hard to learn both English and cake baking, a task he performed with an artisan's care and pride. In time, he had worked his way up to supervise the line. Rob's promotion made Milton "incredibly upset," Lissa recalled, because he considered it a loss of status to have to report to Rob. Milton knew from previous conversations with Trish that he mustn't let his anger explode in the workplace. He was so distressed, however, that he didn't think he could remain calm, Trish said, so he asked to leave and didn't return for the rest of the day.

I am reminded of the way my commanding officer on *Harry W. Hill* doused the flames in fiery interpersonal situations. If I was spitting bullets over something that had happened off the ship, I'd angrily pen a blazing message. But my CO had to first okay its release before it could be sent out over the ship's communication system. Invariably, he would tell me: "Mike, I want you to hold on to this for forty-eight hours. If you still feel the same way in forty-eight hours, then we will send it." Most of the time, after I'd cooled down and looked at the original message, I was relieved that I had been prevented from sending something that would have proved embarrassing. The key is to never do anything in anger, as Milton wisely understood as a result of Trish's previous counseling. A good leader helps employees to save themselves from doing something everyone may come to regret.

Milton and his wife came in to the office the next day at Trish's request to discuss the problem. Trish and Lissa met with the couple for one and a half hours, speaking in a jumble of English and Spanish to work through issues of pride, conflict, misunderstanding, and hurt feelings. It ended, Trish related, with "hugs and kisses all around. He needed that. He couldn't have been happier. But there wasn't any way to get to the other side of that without a lot of time being invested in it."

From Lissa's vantage point, Trish exhibited an eye-opening display of leadership skill. She reassured Milton of her high regard for him and his importance to the company, but bluntly told him he was deluded if he thought he could handle Rob's new job. "This you're not ready for," she said. "Maybe you'll be ready for it some day," Lissa remembers Trish telling Milton, "and if that's something you want to do, these are the things you actually have to change to get there."

Having tried to soft-pedal Milton's shortcomings when she had talked to him the day before, Lissa now saw that constructive feedback combined with caring was the best way to get him back on the team. "Trish is really compelling," Lissa said with obvious admiration. Because of the time and effort she invested, Trish left Milton feeling that she was truly committed to him and appreciated his skills, even if he didn't agree with her decision to promote Rob. "He had faith in Trish," Lissa concluded.

Milton and Rob now have an excellent working relationship. Milton came to understand that underneath Rob's tough-guy exterior is a committed, responsible, creative, and absolutely reliable manager— one who also respects Milton's cake-baking skill and honors him for it. "They both show true respect," Lissa said, and are proud of having repaired their working relationship.

I think Trish did a wonderful job of handling a potentially explosive situation. Many times, an angry outburst can provoke a chain reaction. Suppose Trish had torn into Milton for acting out. Feelings would have been hurt, Milton probably would have viewed Trish as championing what he saw as bad behavior from Rob while discounting Milton's own exemplary performance, and the stage would have been set for an all-out battle. The challenge for us as leaders is always to avoid reacting in anger, even when we think someone is stepping over the line of our authority. Trish not only met that challenge, she also sat everyone down and managed to engineer an extremely positive outcome.

But you know what? I'd expect Milton to act up. He had every right to be upset. In fact, I'd want him to be upset—it shows that he took pride in himself and his work. And if I'd been Trish, I'd have been more upset if Milton hadn't reacted.

During my tour of duty on USS *Benfold*, I made a personnel decision that another officer had every right to be ticked off about. He was—and he came in to tell me about it. Here's what happened:

Navy ships have a collateral duty position called the senior watch officer. Traditionally, it goes to the most senior officer on the ship, the most senior department head (excluding the commanding officer and the executive officer, of course). The position is extremely important and tends to carry a lot of power because the senior watch officer makes all watch assignments, both in port and at sea, for the entire ship.

When we're at sea, for instance, we run two, three, or four section watches, and every watch station must be manned by someone who is technically proficient and qualified to stand the assigned watch. If an accident should occur while someone not officially qualified is standing an assigned watch, all hell breaks loose. The blame falls not on the person who caused the accident, but on the chain of command because it put an unqualified person on watch. So the job itself is not only huge and complex, but it also carries both legal and operational ramifications. Ultimately, the commanding officer has to sign each and every watch bill, certifying that the sailor assigned to each watch is technically proficient and certified to stand it.

It was time for *Benfold*'s senior watch officer to transfer, since his tour of duty was up. Lieutenant Commander K. C. Hill was an enormously talented officer and was one of the original officers when *Benfold* was commissioned. He knew everything about the ship and every person on board, including each sailor's strengths and weaknesses. The really neat thing was that K.C., the combat systems officer, had developed a super infrastructure within his own department to help him

manage the incredibly complex watch system. He was just a phenomenal senior watch officer, better than I ever thought to be.

After K.C., the next most senior officer was Lieutenant Commander Dave Hallisey, who led the operations department. Based on rank,
Dave was in line to become senior watch officer. But if I chose Dave, I
ran the risk of dismantling K.C.'s superb support infrastructure. It was
a thorny problem, and I decided to do something rarely done in the
U.S. Navy: I skipped over the most senior officer and the second-most
senior officer to make Lieutenant John Wade, the third man in line,
the senior watch officer on USS *Benfold*. Why? Because John was replacing K.C. as the combat systems officer, which meant he could take
advantage of the departmental infrastructure devised by K.C. to handle the complexities of the watch system.

Dave Hallisey was understandably upset at being passed over. In his
shoes I would have reacted the same way. So I wasn't surprised or put
off when he came in to talk to me about it. In fact, I was glad to have
the opportunity to explain my reasoning to Dave. First, I assured him
that I had every confidence in him personally and professionally. He
was just as capable as John Wade of managing the watch system. I explained that what gave John the edge was the fact that as combat systems officer, he had inherited K.C.'s phenomenal support system. For
the good of the ship, I had to choose John.

Dave wasn't happy about it, but he understood why I'd done it.
And as the first-rate professional that he was (and still is as the deputy
executive assistant to the secretary of the navy), he supported John
Wade 100 percent. Because Dave handled his disappointment with
such admirable maturity and professionalism, *Benfold* never missed a
beat. We were able to meet all of our obligations.

Sometimes our ego prevents us from supporting a policy we feel
slighted by, and it keeps us from carrying out our mission. At the end
of the day, though, it's got to be about performing the mission in the
best possible manner.

Is it really the best use of a busy CEO's time to spend hours listening to an employee's litany of complaints and frustrations? Might that

time be better spent, for example, massaging big customers and fighting for market share? The answer is no simply because warships and bakeries both would soon lose their competitive edge if they didn't have a happy crew. Show me a leader who truly listens, and I'll show you a workforce that refuses to settle for second best. If you think you're too busy to lend an ear, spend fifteen seconds contemplating Dancing Deer's success.

LESSON: Good leaders care for their people . . .

In the early days at the Dancing Deer bakery, when Suzanne Lombardi's helpers became temperamental and disputatious, she laid down a simple decree: "Don't bake mad. It will ruin the cake." That doctrine has evolved into a wider truth, said Trish, because Dancing Deer "saw that when people were having fun, a lot of good things happened— better ideas came along, productivity and quality went up. Over time it became central to our operating philosophy that if people are happy, it shows in the food. We really believed that, and we still do."

Just as I did on *Benfold*, Trish goes to considerable lengths to keep her people happy. Notable events in employees' lives—birthdays, weddings, the birth of a child, becoming a U.S. citizen—are celebrated, Trish told me. To mark such an occasion, the whole company assembles in the packing room for songs, jokes, light-hearted roasting, and the kind of warm attention that makes a person feel loved and important. Invariably, Trish reminds the partygoers that they are a team, and that "everything everyone is doing is important to our success and to our meeting all of our objectives."

Many companies claim to care about their workers, but most leaders set limits. Trish no doubt has limits too, but they are hard to find. Last year, for instance, at the annual Dancing Deer picnic on an island in Boston Harbor, the head (and staff) of the company's one-woman public relations department broke her ankle in three places during a spontaneous soccer match. Trish put the young woman, Rachel Gordon, onto an ambulance boat and then visited her in the hospital after the picnic ended. Rachel had been enveloped in a cast up to her hip, and was awaiting a needed operation that the doctors decided to put off for three weeks until the swelling subsided. Knowing that Rachel lived alone and had no one to care for her (her parents were in Chicago), Trish said it didn't take her "a fraction of a second to tell Rachel she was coming home with me."

Trish and her two children had to rearrange their house and their lives somewhat to accommodate a houseguest, but Trish saw that as nothing unusual. "I would have done that for anybody here," she said. "I don't know if it was smart, but it was fine with me. It was somebody who needed something, and it had nothing to do with work. It was her personal life, but how do you separate the two?"

Exactly.

LESSON: . . . but caring includes tough love.

Trish likens the management of Dancing Deer to parenting: when things go wrong, leaders, like parents, get through the crisis by looking out for the people they're responsible for. If your employees understand that you are committed to them, it makes them "feel safe and happy even if at that moment they want to strike out at you and be angry," she told me.

But, as Trish realizes, the parental analogy can, and should, be taken only so far. She will never stop being a parent, and loves her children with no strings attached. But in business, a leader's commitment is not unconditional. "People understand that I care deeply for them," she said, "but if someone is not performing and doesn't stretch or do the job over time, then they aren't going to stay here." It wasn't easy, she told me, but she has learned to give the kind of tough, constructive feedback that kept Milton on the team. It adds up to "a contract here where there's a level of mutual respect and caring that is very significant."

Trish feels proud and happy when Dancing Deer people do well, even if they move on to other employers. But, she explained, those feelings are still a step removed from parental sentiments: "It's like going to your goddaughter's graduation. You didn't have that much to do with it, but you're really glad and proud to be there."

While Trish makes a concerted effort to judge her people objectively, never letting her personal concern for them color her appraisal of their talents and skills, she is also willing to adjust their jobs and even the corporate structure to fit their talents. At one point, after the quick departure of a new plant manager who turned out to be ill suited for the job, Lissa asked to take over the newly vacated position. When Trish straightforwardly told Lissa that she lacked the strategic experience or analytic skills needed to handle big-picture issues, such as whether to build a new plant or how to scale it to fit the company five years out, Lissa had to agree.

But that wasn't the end of it. Trish brought aboard a semiretired former chief executive officer to be a part-time operations vice president, and he became Lissa's strategic resource. Trish also hired people to work under Lissa in purchasing, personnel, and operations analysis. "So we built out a whole new level of operations under my supervision," Lissa said.

In the end, Trish gave Lissa most of what she wanted, but in a structure tailored to her abilities and designed to encourage Lissa's growth as a manager.

It's easy for a leader to tell her people what they want to hear. It's also wrong. You can't flatter the weak link in a chain and expect anything but a weakened chain. Always level with your crew. The more truthful you are, the more they respect you and the less they alibi their own flaws.

LESSON: When people criticize you, listen.

From bottom to top, Dancing Deer is a place where people are not afraid to criticize, admit mistakes, and ask for help in fixing them. Lissa told me she never hesitates to confess to Trish that she has caused a problem—though she does try to present an immediate plan for solving it. By the same token, Lissa takes pains to admit her errors to the people who report to her, apologizing and explaining that even though whatever went wrong was her fault, everyone must now pitch in to repair the damage.

Fortunately, Trish works on the same principle. "She and I have had some real knock-down, drag-out conflicts," Lissa said, "and I am so appreciative that she's the kind of person who is willing to take disagreements head-on. Sometimes I worry about my future if I were to move to another company. I've been spoiled by this incredible openness and exchange of ideas."

What Lissa is describing is an ideal leadership situation. Real leaders don't want to run around like buck-naked emperors without a clue as to what's going on in their organizations. They know that people make mistakes, disagree, and have ideas that run counter to their own. But a leader who is worth her salt wants to know all the details, both grand and gory.

There was a time, Lissa recounted, when Dancing Deer was struggling in its efforts to simultaneously roll out groups of new products. Without a system designed to accommodate this new level of sophistication, details such as which cookies to include in a new gift package, whether to add a bow or a ribbon curl, whether enough of the right ribbon was in stock were slipping through the cracks. As a result, new products, the stuff that keeps customers interested, were arriving late to market.

Although Trish constantly complained in management meetings, the issue wasn't being resolved. Finally Lissa blurted out: "It's frustrating. You fuss at people, but it doesn't change them. It seems that the penalty for not doing it right is only to listen to you fuss. Nobody actually has to do it right."

A good many bosses would have exploded, possibly (and wrongly) firing Lissa on the spot. Not Trish. Lissa's outburst started Trish thinking about the lack of accountability. She knew Lissa was right. So Trish came up with a new process for getting all the ducks in a row and holding people accountable for their particular targets. She got the team to buy in to the new religion of working out complete details for every job before letting a product go to the customer. The team took it from there and devised new and better systems that dramatically enhanced performance. The changes were simple ones, really, but Lissa had to speak out before Trish was ready to listen and make the problem a priority.

I always tried to operate the same way on *Benfold*. In our after-action meetings to critique operations, the rule was that anyone could say anything to anyone else without getting gigged for it. The most junior seaman could criticize the captain. It's imperative to have open discussions if you're going to improve things. But I admit that I had to bite my tongue from time to time.

LESSON: The leader has the best voice.

Openness and acceptance of criticism aren't to be confused with weakness. "Trish is the vision for everyone, the life force behind Dancing Deer," according to Lissa. "She makes it a flat organization where you can be part of the decision-making process. But at the same time, she's a really dynamic leader with a will like no human being I've ever met, and there's no doubt who is driving the ship."

Trish herself said her style is evolving; increasingly, she sees herself as the leader of the company rather than "just a person who works really hard and covers a lot of bases." She admitted to being "very demanding—I set high standards and I have learned how to be very direct. There's no question here about who's going to make the final call. I'm in charge, and I don't hesitate to use my authority." And while Trish spreads responsibility around and encourages her people to feel ownership, she insists that in everything that matters, "the voice of Dancing Deer is really me. I'm the best voice here."

Please pause and savor her words: "I'm the best voice here." Is there any better shorthand description for authority? To succeed as a leader, whether in business or on a battleship, you have to believe that your judgment and vision are not just sufficient, but crucial to achieving your goals. I'm not advocating arrogance, and Trish wouldn't either.

It's about being the way finder and the decision maker—literally, the voice of authority.

Underpinning Trish's right—indeed, her need—to speak for the company is an uncanny sense of what's just around the corner, the as-yet-unseen problem or opportunity. "She has an incredible ability to poke holes," Lissa said. "It holds people to a very high level of performance. You've got to be superready because no matter how well you think you've thought it out, Trish is always going to come up with the one question you haven't considered."

Above all, Trish Karter inspires loyalty. "When somebody is that committed to you, you don't want to let her down," Lissa told me. "She's created a very strong corporate culture. We all buy in. We joke a lot about drinking the Kool-Aid as true believers." And in the end, Lissa said, that's because the foremost believer is Trish herself. "She always believes what she's saying. She could sell you almost anything, but it's because she absolutely believes in what she's doing."

TRISH KARTER EMBODIES A FINAL CRUCIAL LESSON I LEARNED in the U.S. Navy: never sail under false colors. When you are 100 percent true to yourself, people will believe in you and follow you anywhere. We all want skippers we can trust—and the employees of Dancing Deer have that in Trish Karter. Her leadership is consistent in all its phases, from concern for pure ingredients through caring for her people to insistence on giving back to the community. She strikes no false notes and has no secret ingredients. It is this sort of integrity that attracts gifted people who love their jobs, and it makes the whole enterprise as straight and level as the leader herself.

LESSONS

Success transcends the bottom line.
Don't become a bottleneck.
Bake teamwork into every cake.

Always be ready for surprise inspections.
Throw a lifeline to struggling crewmates.
Good leaders care for their people . . .
. . . but caring includes tough love.
When people criticize you, listen.
The leader has the best voice.

CHAPTER 3

CEO Roger Valine Demands
a Great Deal from Everyone—
and Gives a Great Deal Back

*Perks and paternalism haven't gone out of style at an eye-care
benefits provider where the CEO's penchant for managing by the
Golden Rule produces satisfied employees and glittering results.*

SEEMINGLY GONE THE WAY OF TAIL FINS AND DOO-WOP
harmonies is the fifties notion of spending an entire career at one great
corporation that feels like family—a paternal place that guarantees
solid jobs, friends, and pride. Plus amazing fringe benefits. If you're
too young to remember such relics, they were called free health insurance, month-long vacations, and lifetime pensions.

In our brave new world of outsourcing and virtual companies, the
old model sounds as quaint as the manual typewriter. So why did our
parents love it so? Because it was okay back then to be a company man.
More than okay. Year after year the hardworking loyalty you gave to
XYZ Inc. was faithfully returned in the form of security and serenity,
prime values of the day. Few XYZ lifers had the slightest clue that information technology would soon change everything; the company's
future was shrinking by the week.

XYZ and companies like it have long passed into memory, and if
you stumbled on a replica in some remote corner of America, it would
be like finding archaeological treasure, a corporate Pompeii buried in
the sands of time.

Okay, cover your eyes. I have a surprise.

Now open—voilà.

Meet Vision Service Plan (VSP), the nation's biggest provider of eye-care benefit plans, covering everything from simple exams to advanced surgery. Based in Rancho Cordova, California, ten miles east of Sacramento, VSP is a nonprofit network of thousands of eye doctors serving twenty-one thousand employers and their employees coast to coast. It now covers thirty-eight million people—one in eight Americans, including one third of all Californians. VSP's revenues have multiplied many times over in the past three decades, going from ten million dollars in 1973 to two billion dollars in 2003, a sum that clearly qualifies it as big business.

But the real eye-opener, so to speak, is something else. VSP is an almost peerless embodiment of the old paternal corporation, where contented people worked hard but worked to live rather than lived to work. In ranking the one hundred best places to work in America, *Fortune* magazine listed VSP seventeenth last year, up from the forty-fifth spot *Fortune* first awarded the company five years ago. So many job hunters yearn to join VSP's mere two thousand employees that the company has to disappoint more than twenty-seven thousand applicants every year.

The kudos for VSP's rousing success surely belong to every one of those two thousand employees. Yes, but the lion's share goes to the company's presiding inspirer, Roger Valine, a fifty-five-year-old sociologist turned chief executive who sees no reason to differentiate between the often clashing concepts of company man and family man. Roger Valine strives to exemplify both, and VSP is a wondrous place because of it.

Roger is a balding, big-boned man who grew up on 340 acres of working farmland near Sacramento, where his grandparents settled after emigrating from Portugal's Azores Islands in 1860. When he was only ten, Roger was big enough to help grown-ups harvest the farm's crops—alfalfa, barley, beans, corn, safflower, sugar beets. Along the way, he absorbed his parents' work ethic and managerial ideas. Joe and Lorraine Valine were collaborators, not controllers. "You couldn't tell from my father or mother who was the laborer or who was the client,"

Roger told me. "My parents were very respectful of people, not because of wealth. They were centered on the quality of the person. Were they true to their word? Were they good to other people?" The son also noticed how much his own performance depended on Joe and Lorraine's respect: "Even though I always tried to do the best I could, I knew I stretched more when I was treated well. It made sense to me to have that kind of environment at VSP."

Young Roger showed an early taste for challenges. At the age of eight, for example, he visited the California State Fair with his mother and passed a booth that invited fairgoers to throw a softball hard enough to knock over a pyramid of five steel milk bottles. Fee: fifty cents a throw. Forget it, his mother said. The bottles are cemented; it's a gimmick. Besides, you're not strong enough. But Roger insisted. His mother finally paid fifty cents to shut him up. He promptly heaved a strike that demolished the pyramid and won him a prize teddy bear. The real prize was Roger's discovery that can-do kids can confound can't-do grown-ups.

One of Roger's biggest challenges as a young man was how to find a career in which he could gain major success without shortchanging family life. To that end, he chose to avoid the distractions of New York or Los Angeles and remain instead in Sacramento, his home turf. A growing interest in human behavior led him to major in sociology at the nearby campus of California State University, from which he graduated in 1972. And right in Sacramento he happened upon VSP, a curious company founded in 1955 by six optometrists in Oakland who pooled their expertise, marketed it to labor unions, and formed the country's first nonprofit eye-care insurance plan. A decade later, buoyed by its credibility as a rapidly expanding network of ophthalmologists, VSP became a national model of its kind and moved to better quarters in Sacramento.

The job opportunity offered to Roger Valine in 1973 was as a management trainee, hardly a blood racer and, in practice, more a matter of selling than of managing. But besides being local, the company was imbued with an appealing philosophy. What immediately drew

Roger to VSP was John O'Donnell, the company's founding chief executive, who seemed passionate about encouraging employees to balance their lives between work and family. "I was very impressed with Mr. O'Donnell," Roger recalled. "A career was and is very important to me, but not more than my family. So I chose VSP because its corporate headquarters was in Sacramento, and I thought I could move up in the business without having to move my family."

Roger is enormously and publicly devoted to his family—his wife of thirty-one years, Marie, and their two daughters, one son, and two grandchildren. These special people even take precedence over his Harley-Davidson motorcycle, a Heritage Softail that Marie gave him in 1993 and that he regularly rides to work at VSP. Some H-D addicts reverse this preference, but Roger always puts family first—so much so that he distinguishes good years from bad in part by what's happened in his family, and he describes these highlights and lowlights with candor and humor in an annual address to VSP staffers.

In a company where the *grand fromage* is called Roger, or even Rog, no one seems to find his easy informality hard to take. One week's news flash reported his daughter Anne's accident in San Francisco, which required Dad to drive down and retrieve her from a firehouse. With no lack of parental pride, Roger didn't forget to mention that Anne had cooked dinner for the firemen to show her appreciation for their kindness after her accident. It was a photo op, and Roger had the goods to prove it.

Roger says his parents instilled in him the key to managing VSP: "You treat people the way you want to be treated." The result seems to be a mix of hard and soft—a relentless push to boost VSP's performance, combined with down-home informality and systematic caring about each employee's well-being. But don't be misled. Roger Valine is no sentimental sucker. Family values shape his life, but improving VSP *is* his life.

There is a reason why Roger Valine marched steadily upward at VSP, from trainee in 1973 to salesman to senior vice president to chief executive in 1992. There is a reason why VSP under Roger Valine has grown in twelve years from a California company with five hundred million dollars in annual sales to a national organization with optical labs, a frame company, offices in twenty-five cities, and sales of two billion dollars, a figure that he predicts will hit three billion dollars by 2011.

The reason is that Roger Valine demands a great deal from everyone, beginning with himself, while giving a great deal back. New hires are given specific, written objectives, plus all the resources needed to carry them out. At year's end, they are subjected to a tough performance review. This process is repeated every subsequent year. It's not hostile, and is actually designed to be supportive. "We do everything we can to make everybody succeed," said Walter Grubbs, the company's vice president for human resources. "We don't want to be the kind of company that chews people up and spits them out."

VSP may not spit, but neither does it swallow poor performance. It does not hesitate to fire those who fail to deliver. Roughly three hundred of the company's two thousand employees leave every year, a third of them after being fired. This isn't as harsh as it may sound. Five hundred employees work in two call centers, a job with typically high turnover rates; VSP's total firings are actually on the modest side by industry standards. And given the company's Golden Rule philosophy of management, the firings are not capricious or hasty. VSP jobs are so hotly sought and highly valued that its employees strive mightily to keep them. This, after all, is a company with liberal flextime for working parents, a twenty-five-hundred dollar yearly grant for anyone who pursues off-hour schooling, paid time off to do volunteer work, a yearly bonus of one week's salary, profit sharing, and a monthly Cake Day, which celebrates all current birthdays with a wide array of tasty offerings.

It's also a company where the boss has next to his office an "airplane" room, in which he's installed two refurbished American Airlines first-class seats. Roger says he thinks best riding on airplanes, so he tries to replicate that feeling at sea level. Faced with big-company problems, he slips into the airplane room, sinks into his grounded seats, and ponders solutions. Characteristically, Roger doesn't reserve this CEO perk for himself alone. Not long ago, for instance, he lent the airplane room to a courting VSP couple so the man could pop the question and they could envision themselves at thirty-five thousand feet on their honeymoon flight.

Roger Valine has come a long way as a leader. "When I first arrived here," Walter Grubbs remembered, "he tended to jump right into something at the beginning. He has a kind of fix-it personality. He would say where he thought we should go, how we should resolve a problem right away, and people tended to stand by silently. Over time, he got concerned that people were agreeing with him without expressing their own opinions. He realized he needed those opinions. So he began working hard to bite his tongue at meetings and wait for others to weigh in before he did." It worked, Grubbs said, albeit slowly.

The upshot was that Roger absorbed one of the basic rules of leadership—don't assume you know it all, or you won't ever discover what you don't know. Leaders need charisma, yes, but not so much that they stifle alternate views by the sheer force of their personalities. Successful leaders reach out for others' ideas and insights. They never stop listening and learning.

How his policies may affect the workforce is perhaps the one question that Roger most often asks his executive team. "In every business decision, his first filter is always the people, what it will do to them," said another chief executive who knows him well. "It's a remarkable quality that not a lot of businesspeople have."

Roger pursues a decision's aftermath even more vigorously. In his constant quest for feedback, he keeps reaching out to take the company pulse, frequently joining VSP lunchers for a latest-news fix in the employees' cafeteria. He is famous for being approachable in the elevator, especially if you catch him in the lobby of VSP's new headquarters and ride up with him all six floors to his office. Besides informal chats as he ambles around the premises, Roger has assigned key people to notify him quickly about the staff's pro or con reactions to whatever he's said, done, or decided. And four times a year, he invites a dozen employees from different parts of the company to join him in a focus group aimed at identifying significant issues he should resolve or get cracking on.

A distillation of these discussions becomes the agenda for Roger's twice-yearly presentations to the entire workforce. These are big, carefully inclusive events that bring together all those he considers crucial stakeholders in VSP's future, meaning everybody. By no coincidence, the gatherings resemble a cross between a family reunion and a company's annual stockholders' meeting.

Right now, VSP's future is much on Roger's mind because he will retire in January of 2008, capping a one-company career of nearly thirty-five years. And there is unfinished business. VSP faces growing competition from a bevy of imitators in the eye-care benefits business, partly because its value proposition has been so successful.

Roger is equally concerned about identifying, and recommending to his board, the ideal successor for his job. He strongly prefers an in-house candidate. For one thing, the familial culture he's created at VSP would be best understood and preserved by one who's steeped in it. Even a sympathetic outsider might come to see the company as a paternalistic throwback ripe for a hard-nosed makeover. A new CEO might also disagree with Roger Valine's leadership style, which includes, for example, his painfully learned willingness to seek contrary opinions and to delegate projects he once couldn't stop himself from micromanaging.

The only certainty is that his style of leadership works magnificently for Roger. He has created a team whose quarterback seems to throw a half-dozen balls at once to receivers all over the field, urging each to run for the goal. At VSP, the most unsung people are likely to qualify for the company's annual Gold Vision Award, having exemplified Victor Hugo's maxim that "initiative is doing the right thing without being told." One woman, for example, was responsible for delivering VSP manuals and newsletters to some eighteen thousand doctors across the country. On her own, she quietly changed bindings and paper weights, saving the company three hundred thousand dollars a year in the process.

Then there's the story of Patricia Cochran, now VSP's chief financial officer. Back in 1997, when President Bill Clinton held a summit meeting on volunteerism, Roger was invited to attend and he brought along Patricia, who had long mixed community work with her day job at VSP. Out of the White House meeting came the notion that VSP might explore a charity program to provide free eye care to uninsured children. To her surprise, Roger turned to Patricia and said, "I want you to see if you can develop this program for us."

Never had she tackled anything so complex. No matter. Patricia succeeded admirably. Called Sight for Students, her program has already raised and spent nearly fifty million dollars on free eye exams and eyeglasses for more than 250,000 uninsured, low-income children. Roger's vision not only transformed Patricia's life, but gave vision—literally—to a quarter-million children whose chances for success in school and beyond were hugely multiplied.

Roger Valine's successor at VSP may well find him a hard act to follow. But many of us will rightly wish to follow his prescriptives for leadership. Among the lessons to be gleaned from Roger's extraordinarily successful style of leadership:

LESSON: Lead the charge by giving charge.

During Roger's first years with VSP, the business was small enough that senior managers were also hands-on managers, ready and willing to make most decisions. That was fine with Roger. But when he became chief executive in 1992, it became clear to him that a new approach was urgently needed. The company was growing so fast it was "about to explode," he told me, which distracted his team from making good decisions. Roger himself was overworked, devoting more than eighty hours a week to VSP. Fed up, Marie Valine questioned her husband's priorities and strongly suggested that he needed to do the same. "She was absolutely right," he said.

Roger switched his leadership style. "I realized I had very competent people working here," he told me, "and they could probably make better decisions than I could in their areas of responsibility. I made a very open move to get out of the way of their decision making. The result actually helped our company grow even faster." For instance, after championing the formation of Altair Eyewear in 1992 to help manage the rising cost of frames, Roger handed over day-to-day responsibility to a hard-charging young manager who had caught his eye. In just a few years, the Altair start-up has grown to be one of the top-ten frame companies in the nation, Roger told me. Just as important to Roger, though, was the way his new leadership philosophy transformed his personal life. "It allowed me to have a healthier balance in my life—to know my children as they were growing up instead of suddenly finding out too late that they were off in college somewhere and didn't know me."

That said, Roger does put some limits on delegating. When a decision involves more than five million dollars, it gets kicked up to the next level of authority. Also, he won't countenance a decision at any level that threatens his company's well-tended relationships with its member doctors and clients. "When you're dealing with something that addresses who you are as an organization or what you're known for or stand for," he said firmly, "that would be something that nobody had better mess with."

Moreover, as Roger told me, leaders who decide to give charge rather than take it need to recognize that "there can be multiple ways of arriving at a successful strategy." He looks for opportunities to "let people have their head," especially those capable of carrying through on a decision. Patricia Cochran's development of Sight for Students, the children's eye-care program, is a prime example.

Roger has even learned to sit back when his aides propose making a decision that he himself would not have suggested. "Give it a chance," he says. "The risks aren't all that great, and sometimes their idea is better than I thought, or even better than mine."

As I learned in the navy, if you keep denying people's ideas because you have a slight preference for something else, you create a bigger problem for yourself. As much as you might try to tell your crew that you appreciate their input, they start clamming up, afraid of being shot down if they suggest anything. You lose the information and experience they have to contribute.

LESSON: High-tech demands more delegation of duties than ever.

Back in 1982, when I became antisubmarine warfare officer aboard USS *Albert David,* the Internet was unknown, and we had very little fancy technology. Navy life was simple. We dealt with only one mission area at a time, and the captain could micromanage everything.

Computers back then were very primitive. The one we used to program gunnery was an old analog machine. You punched in the coordinates of the target and then watched its dials spinning as it made its calculations. You could leave and have lunch while it figured things out.

Fast-forward to USS *Benfold* fifteen years later. Reams of information bombarded us. New technology allowed us to handle six mission areas at a time. In a single moment I could shoot the ship's guns, launch its cruise missiles, fire the torpedoes, control aircraft in flight, search for enemy communications, and direct the boarding of ships going into and out of Iraq. What is more, once you have this ability at your fingertips, your chain of command insists you use it more and more effectively.

Technology allows us to man our ships with 75 percent of the people we needed twenty years ago. Conversely, we now have to do six times as much work with 25 percent fewer people. And one person can no longer control it all. Yet some people cling to the old model, and while they may still be able to micromanage one or two mission areas, the other four are likely to fall apart.

People slip into a rut doing things the old way because it's so comfortable. Our fathers were able to lead in a command-and-control style because they had the luxury of being able to focus on one thing at a time and get decent results. It doesn't work that way anymore in the military or in business. You are constantly bombarded with bits of information that demand decisions, and if you don't develop a team to handle certain areas for you, you're going to get so bogged down in detail that you'll have no time left to actually lead. Before long, your operations will begin to show the effects of your neglect. Disaster is just around the corner.

I don't mean to brag, but *Benfold*'s performance was peerless in just about every mission area. Even though our different responsibilities required different levels of skill, we were up to the challenge.

On a ship like ours, the most complex war-fighting position is the job of antiair warfare coordinator (AAWC). Everything moves at warp speed in air defense—troublesome scenarios pop up out of nowhere—and the AAWC has to have superior motor and verbal skills to man the console that tracks potentially hostile aircraft.

Imagine yourself manning your console, your hand and fingers manipulating a little ball that tracks incoming targets at the same time you are reading out all the parameters of these targets. When an invader appears on the screen, the AAWC must simultaneously consider speed, direction, and identification codes, while also vectoring one of our own aircraft to intercept as quickly as possible. At the same time, you're using the R/T net to tell everyone in your battle group what's going on and giving them directions. Your hands are flying around the computer console while you talk furiously to dozens of people who depend on your skill and speed to keep them alive. If your attention wavers for a nanosecond, you're behind in the air game and someone in your battle group may be dead.

To say the situation is intense and complex doesn't do it justice. Few people are wired for the job, including me. I just don't have the dexterity. The people who do are part of the Nintendo generation. They grew up playing video games, developing the hand-eye coordination needed to control real video games in the sky, while I grew up learning antisubmarine warfare. Here you stand around a big plotting table that shows submarine contacts and where they're headed. The pattern develops slowly over hours or days. You yawn as you sip your coffee. You can take a break to grab another cup of coffee or a can of Coke and not miss a thing. That's not to say the submarine mission doesn't demand a tremendous amount of skill. It does. It's just that the submarine mission moves at a far slower pace.

Nevertheless, as captain, it was my job to staff each of our six mission areas with their own warfare coordinators. These people relayed what was going on in their individual areas to the captain (me), and I had to keep tabs on all six areas without getting lost in details. My manning profile demanded that I have a mix of both commissioned officers and chief petty officers in the warfare-coordinator positions. But I didn't have enough of either group to handle these vital jobs. What to do?

Chief petty officers are developed in a step-by-step process that enlisted people go through to master higher skill levels aboard ship and to pass the exams required to officially attain the higher ratings. Junior commissioned officers come from the Naval Academy, the Reserve Officers Training Corps (ROTC), or Officer Candidate School (OCS). When they first come aboard, they know nothing about war fighting and traditionally start out handling a division and doing administrative tasks. As far as I'm concerned, that's a waste.

I wanted officers whose war-fighting skills are up to speed ASAP. On *Benfold* we had our own way of handling new junior officers. First we figured out which warfare mission a new officer had the most aptitude for, and then we immersed her or him in an intense three- to four-month program to get the officer mission qualified right off the bat. Once they were qualified, we gave them a division to lead. *Benfold's* way was completely upside down from the usual navy way.

One reason warfare coordinators typically come from the ranks of commissioned officers and chief petty officers is that they deal directly by radio with higher ranks. Each coordinator has a counterpart aboard the flagship commanding the battle group, and each mission area reports to a major warfare commander on the flagship who supervises that particular duty for all the group's warships. A stickler for navy protocol would certainly expect these ship-to-ship conversations to be handled by people with enough rank to talk easily to commodores and admirals.

On *Benfold* we had an unorthodox approach. I couldn't wait the twelve to fifteen years it takes for enlisted people to become chief petty officers. Instead, we targeted talented junior enlisted people. Today's navy is full of extremely smart second- or third-class petty officers with four or five years of service. As I saw it, if they had the aptitude and the desire, there was nothing to keep them from becoming warfare coordinators.

Which leads me to a neat story. We were in the Persian Gulf, boarding vessels going into and out of Iraq to search for illegal contraband. For this duty we reported to Commodore Mike Duffy. He was tough. He could rip your throat out over the radio if you didn't measure up. *Benfold* became his prized ship because we had cross-trained so many people and thus could handle several missions at once. The commodore decided to come for a visit. He wanted to see how we did it.

Duffy walked into the combat information center, and I pointed out the maritime interdiction coordinator. He looked at me and said, "This can't be right. He's a second-class petty officer, an enlisted man." I said, "Yes, sir. What's the problem?" Duffy growled, "I've only seen officers and chief petty officers standing this watch. You mean to tell me I've been talking to an enlisted man on that radio?" He was so befuddled he could barely speak.

I had lunch with Mike Duffy recently, and he brought up that story. He said he still couldn't get over his shock when he boarded *Benfold* and discovered that the mission coordinator talking to him and his staff on the radio was a lowly enlisted man. Well, Duffy's initial shock eventually turned to unabashed delight. It can't hurt the navy if the smartest young men and women get the most demanding jobs, no matter what rank they are.

LESSON: Allow room for mistakes, and encourage people to tell you when they screw up.

For give-charge leadership to work, your people have to know that a botched decision won't cost them their jobs. "You've got to create an environment where making a mistake isn't so terrifying," Roger told me. "We all make mistakes. But if we keep stretching and trying new things, we'll make far more good decisions than someone who always just wants to play it safe."

What Roger relies on is the expectation that the people making decisions will let him know if they're worried about possible outcomes. Otherwise, he has no desire for colleagues "who feel they need to talk to three different people or have four different memos supporting their position before they act." People who worry more about covering their asses than making the right decision just slow down an organization. "There's not enough time in the day to do that in a business of our size," Roger said.

He has a good system for maintaining his own accountability to VSP's board. "We have four board meetings a year," he said, "and in between those we have four committee meetings a year. There is ample opportunity to give the board status reports on what's going on or how we're doing." In a normal week, Roger said, he leaves at least three or four voice mails for the company's chairman, just to keep him in the loop in case some issue heats up. That way, if need be, the chairman already has a head start on coming to grips with an issue. "I think people like that," Roger mused. "There's no hidden agenda. There's no worry about who's not telling what to whom. I believe he trusts me and knows that if there's anything relevant, he will know about it." That is Roger's recipe for creating mutual trust. The chairman doesn't feel the need to micromanage or get more involved because he's already receiving a satisfactory level of information.

Thinking about Roger's approach reminded me, though, that a leader who puts other people in charge, even when it's the right thing to do, can run into unseen complications. Sometimes the confidence you develop in your people can lead them to become dangerously overconfident. I should know because it happened to my best department head on *Benfold*. This is a phenomenal officer who should, and probably will, make admiral one day. But in this particular instance, he bit off more than he could chew.

A piece of equipment used in his department broke two weeks before we needed it for an antisubmarine warfare exercise. Because he never missed a commitment and knew that I had the utmost confidence in his abilities, he thought he could handle the problem without telling me. Two weeks later, just before the exercise was to begin, he came to me and said we couldn't participate because the equipment was broken. I asked him how long he'd known. Two weeks, he said. With the passage of every one of those fourteen days, he decreased my ability to help him solve the problem—say, by borrowing the equipment from another ship. He took away my options, and you never want to infringe on the options of your superiors.

The thing is, nothing is perfect. Stuff is going to break. It's not a sign of incompetence to report the situation—if you do it in time to fix it. Bad news does not improve with age. You have to make that perfectly clear to your crew.

I looked this young officer in the eye and said very calmly, "In my whole career, I've never been more disappointed with someone than I am with you right now." It hit him right where I wanted it to—in his gut. He was visibly upset. I didn't raise my voice. If you yell at people, tear their heads off, they're apt not to bring you bad news in the future, and you can't afford that. The tack I took with him was that he had let me and his shipmates down. He felt awful, and he never did it again.

This officer went on to command his own ship, and he imparted this very important lesson to his people: You've got to keep me informed. I won't shoot you if you bring me bad news, but I will shoot you if you delay telling me, thus inhibiting my ability to help you fix the problem. When stuff happens and people keep it to themselves, it tells you that you are not running a shipshape ship.

LESSON: Soft heart, hard ass.

For five straight years—from 1998 to 2003—VSP has ranked high on *Fortune*'s list of the best companies to work for in the United States. Part of its popularity derives from the wide range of benefits it offers, from health care to flextime for working parents to bonuses and profit sharing. Roger's organizing principle for managing people is, quite simply, the Golden Rule.

Respect for others is part of Roger's birthright. His parents, he told me, treated people "with dignity regardless of their social standing." He often talks about seeing his father on one end of an irrigation pipe and a migrant worker on the other, and about the respect and consideration, not to mention coordination, that went back and forth between them. They relied on each other to get the job done. "Why shouldn't this business be operated the same way?" he wondered.

"But I don't want to kid you," he told me. "I don't want you to think this is just a nice little organization that doesn't have pressure, because it certainly does. We have very high expectations of performance. We also have a little higher rate of involuntary turnover than most companies."

At the end of the day, results rule. On *Benfold,* being liked by my crew was not one of my goals. Being respected was. I wanted the crew to have confidence that I could lead them and keep them safe in return for their going all out to make us the best ship afloat. When your people lack confidence in you, they tend to slack off. "If the captain's not going all out, why should we?" becomes the mind-set.

So doing nice things isn't just about being nice. It's about making your people more productive so they can meet those high expectations you've set for them. If you provide day care on the premises, for example, you free up busy parents to focus on their work because they don't have to worry about running off to pick up their kids before their care provider closes for the day. The same goes for on-premises dry-cleaning services or exercise facilities; you're giving back time to your people that they can spend on you. That's why I call perks performance enhancers. By recognizing that your people have outside pressures and by helping them to cope, you enable your crew to deliver better performance for you.

One of the unfortunate realities of navy bases is their waterside locations, which means sky-high rents that sailors can't afford. Sailors have to move inland where housing is cheaper (and lousier). So they have long commutes. Traditionally, a ship's working hours are from 0730 to 1630. So when sailors are in home port, they constantly get stuck in traffic during peak rush hours. Low pay, poor housing, and traffic jams—it's a depressing combination for sailors.

We couldn't do much about the pay or the housing, but we did help *Benfold* sailors avoid some of the traffic problems around San Diego. We changed the working day to begin at 0630 and end with lunch at 1330. That gave us seven uninterrupted hours of work. We bypassed the morning and evening commuting problems, and got more work done because we didn't interrupt momentum by breaking for lunch. Typically, people have a hard time getting settled back in when they return from lunch, so a good portion of the afternoon hours are wasted anyway. Our sailors also appreciated having time to run their errands in the afternoon.

In every organization, leaders have to maintain a balance between "making nice" with employees and holding them accountable for their performance. Finding your own point of equilibrium is one of your most important responsibilities as a leader. If you set the bar so high that it's unreachable, you may be rewarded with people who give up as they get frustrated. The challenge is to determine what's humanly achievable with the resources at your disposal, and then to put the processes in place that will get you there.

At VSP, Roger has carved out the perfect space between being a soft-hearted guy and a hard-assed manager, as evidenced by the company's extremely low (9 percent) voluntary turnover rate and its impressive business results. VSP boasts a five-year growth rate of 100 percent.

Roger says his essential goal is "to have great people working for us who will want to be with us forever." To encourage a kind of loyalty that is increasingly rare in the workplace today, he treats employees with respect, rewards them generously with cash and perks, and recognizes that sometimes their personal needs should take precedence over their professional duties.

In the last category, I put his insistence that employees must take their annual vacations to spend time with their families. He also encourages parents to take time off to watch their children pitch a Little League game or perform in a school play. If child-care or parent-care responsibilities weigh heavily on a member of Roger's crew, they can take advantage of a flextime schedule. To cut down on after-work errands and speed employees home at day's end, VSP has a dry cleaner, car wash, and convenience store on site at its Sacramento headquarters. It even has a program that enables employees to get eye-care benefits for friends and extended family, and one that offers low-rate real estate loans along with pet insurance and legal assistance.

"What I think makes our people really give a little extra to the company," Roger told me, "is knowing that the company is always going to give it to them when they need it." Or *want* it, he might have added. Besides the health benefits, bonuses, and the like, that its employees might need, VSP also provides things they might merely have a hankering for, such as a basketball court, picnic area, and putting green.

As I mentioned earlier, everyone at VSP, top to bottom, is on a first-name basis. When Roger lunches in the cafeteria, he sits down with frontline employees to find out what's going on in their personal and work lives. Once a year, In-Touch Day sends all managers into the workplace to observe and chat with frontline people, soliciting their ideas and complaints, getting to know people from all departments.

At Thanksgiving, senior managers serve lunch to employees. There's an annual dinner dance, an annual family picnic, the monthly Cake Day celebrations of birthdays and anniversaries, and special celebrations whenever the company achieves something big. In 1998, for example, when revenues reached one billion dollars, VSP threw a Thanks-a-Billion Party. Red carpets awaited employees when they walked into their offices, champagne flowed, and toasts soared. Roger gave a gracious speech, thanking the entire workforce. "Those things are fun and break the monotony of work," he said, "and they don't cost much. It's so easy for management to be critical of things, and I fall prey to that myself. So we look for ways to praise good work and inspire people to keep doing it."

But VSP is hardly a resort for preretirees. Roger's concern for his employees' well-being is exceeded only by his insistence that they do superb work. Accountability begins the moment they're hired and given specific objectives with benchmarks to measure their progress. At their first annual performance review, they're told how well they did. And at any time along the way, an underperformer is expected to consult one of the company's human resources counselors to ascertain if his problems are the result of having the wrong tools, bad information, or his own inability or disinclination to do the work.

The point is, employees are responsible for their own careers. The company is a partner in the process, supplying the requisite tools and knowledge. But in the final analysis, a VSP employee must take charge of his or her progress, get help when needed, and seek training and other educational opportunities to improve skills.

VSP bonuses are far from automatic; they are determined by performance levels, both group and individual. Salespeople aren't given quotas; they choose a dollar figure goal that represents a stretch, but their bonus will, in the end, be based on how much they sell. Exceeding your one-million-dollar stretch goal by another one million, for example, gets you less than setting a stretch goal of four million dollars and only reaching three million. As Roger put it, "If your system is based just on achieving or exceeding your goal, human nature would have you start setting your sights lower."

For frontline employees and managers, their bonus depends on whether the company meets its goals in two basic areas. The first concerns satisfaction levels among VSP's major corporate and government clients, its doctors who deliver the vision care, and the millions of patients who receive that care. The second area covers the efficiency level of the corporation—not an individual's team or department but the entire organization.

When goals are not met, checks don't get mailed. If there is a goal of reducing operating costs per claim by 2 percent a year, for example, and that doesn't happen, no one receives the efficiency-related bonus, which represents 50 percent of the total possible bonus. "If you have something that's tied just to individuals or their departments," Roger explained, "you can have a problem. It tempts departments not to stretch to help other departments because it could be detrimental to their own personal bonus, even though it might be the best thing for the company as a whole. We want to keep people focused on the company as a whole."

VSP employees know the company expects their best, and if their best doesn't measure up to the organization's high standards, they know they may not keep their jobs. "If someone isn't operating at a very high level," Roger said, "we certainly will tell them about that and offer them additional training. But if they turn down the training or just can't cut the mustard, they'll be asked to leave. I think that's fair and right, and it keeps our company healthy."

So that's how Roger Valine and his company balance between soft heart and hard ass. They provide all sorts of perks; they treat employees with respect and affection and nurture their careers. But they expect and demand a high degree of commitment and superior performance in return.

I think it's a fair bargain and, apparently, so do the twenty-seven thousand people who apply to fill only a few hundred job openings each year.

LESSON: Go fish.

In his earlier days at VSP, Roger Valine spent a lot of time interviewing and hiring sales personnel. He no longer does much of that, but his ideas about assessing job candidates permeate the company's standards. He sees hiring as the most important single process required for a successful business. "We really take extra time—anywhere from three to seven weeks more than the average company—to find the best people, far more time than the average company," he told me. "We find those who are driven, who have integrity, who have a team aspect in their thinking as opposed to always thinking about what's in it for them."

Roger sometimes begins an interview by going over the candidate's résumé and asking questions to determine why certain decisions were made. He tries to get a sense of whether the person is answering his questions honestly or just providing a rehearsed response. Is she a self-starter? For sales jobs, in particular, Roger notes whether he or the candidate is doing all the talking and who is trying to control the interview. "Is this person trying to manage me as much as I'm trying to manage her?" he asks himself. If the answer is yes, that's a point in the applicant's favor.

Another favorable sign is a candidate who asks specific questions about VSP—its major competitors, its market share, its five-year outlook. "Those are questions from someone who is looking to do more than collect a paycheck over the next year," Roger said.

Assuming the candidate passes muster on all these matters, Roger then engages in a singular mental exercise. "I ask myself what it would be like to spend forty-eight hours alone with this person on a fishing trip with no TV or other distractions. Would it be fun, or would I be jumping off the side of the boat within a few hours?"

The object of the exercise is to arrive at a reasoned judgment about the candidate's ability to establish a relationship with another person in a relatively short period of time. That is a most necessary skill in the vision-benefits business, where corporate and government clients must be fully convinced of a company's professionalism before they sign a contract so important to their employees' well-being.

Some people Roger has interviewed have had "a whole lot of the right kind of skills and background," he said, "but I had to pass them over because they flunked the fishing-trip test. Right or wrong, that's been one way we've built up our sales staff, and you have to admit that they've done great work for us."

Roger's "go fish" idea is a good one when it comes to certain occupations. For a sales force you obviously need outgoing, friendly people, the sort who instinctively establish good relationships with everybody, notably customers. But I can think of other work environments where backslappers are just the opposite of what's needed. Certain technology-oriented jobs, for instance, require intense concentration and a more sedate atmosphere. At the end of the day, you need to determine what kind of people fit best into your workplace and hire accordingly. The point is to find people who not only get the job done but also do it in a superb fashion.

On my ship we had assorted sailors and officers I wouldn't want to go fishing with, but that didn't mean they weren't phenomenal performers. Your particular job requirements will determine who fits in, but, like Roger, you will need to spend some time figuring out your specific criteria.

Whatever your particular professional requirements, though, I would encourage you to make every effort to put together the most diverse group possible. Hiring clones is an idea limiter. I think *Benfold* was a better place because of the wide range of people on board. But bringing together people of various ethnicities and experiences doesn't mean that everyone must want to pal around together. You only have to respect each other and work well together as a team.

LESSON: Put success into succession.

Successful leaders aren't quitters, which makes it difficult for them when the time comes to step down. That is particularly true for those who have only recently reached a high-level job. No sooner have you begun to feel comfortable and in command of your workplace than you have to start thinking about moving out and finding a replacement. But the sad truth is that if you want to fulfill your responsibility as a leader of your organization and its people, you have no choice. The hunt for a successor should start at least two to three years before your retirement date.

At Vision Service Plan, Roger Valine takes his responsibility for finding the right successor very seriously. He began his succession planning by talking with his vice presidents and a handful of other people around the company, asking for their ideas as to what would be important to VSP's success over the next decade or so. He also wanted to know what kind of person would be appropriate to lead VSP in that new environment—what skills and personal characteristics would be needed? (The qualities Roger's colleagues described—trustworthy, hardworking with good communication and strategic skills, and passionate about the business—sounded remarkably like the man the new CEO will replace.)

Roger has continued his conversations with his top aides and has solicited from them the names of potential CEO candidates within the organization. He also asked them to list each candidate's strengths and weaknesses.

His attention to finding his own replacement mirrors Roger's and VSP's intense interest in succession planning. "We take it very seriously," he told me. Every two years, vice presidents and directors are asked to name people in the company who might be either a short-term or long-term replacement. The immediate goal is to have some potential fill-ins ready in case a vice president or a director becomes temporarily unable to work or moves on to another job outside the company. But Roger has another motive as well: "It's one of the ways we find out who our folks think are the up-and-comers. We try to give these people a bit more varied experience because most likely they're going to be some of the future leaders of our business."

Thinking about your future retirement may be unpleasant, but the alternative is far worse. No responsible leader would want to leave his or her crew floundering, with no one at the helm who can keep everyone focused on the enterprise's goals. It's something like drawing up your will—a disagreeable task that no responsible person can avoid.

———

ROGER VALINE COMBINES THE BEST OF THE OLD-STYLE paternalistic employer with a twenty-first-century realization that to-day's business milieu is an unforgiving taskmaster that demands superlative performance from all who seek to compete. His basic decency and respect for those who toil to make his Vision Service Plan a growing success have led him to protect and reward his employees to an uncommon degree. Yet like a good father, he won't abide bad behavior. As VSP powers ahead, Roger Valine is proving that the old ways may indeed be the best ways.

LESSONS

Lead the charge by giving charge.
High-tech demands more delegation
of duties than ever.
Allow room for mistakes, and encourage
people to tell you when they screw up.
Soft heart, hard ass.
Go fish.
Put success into succession.

CHAPTER 4

Captain Al Collins Follows to Lead

So you're a black kid from rural Georgia
with no money, no contacts, no prospects.
Is that gonna hold you down? Only if you let it.

AL COLLINS GREW UP IN WARNER ROBINS, GEORGIA, A
cotton-picking hamlet of thirty-five thousand souls, half of them
black and all of them broke nearly ten months of every year. His
mother kept house; his father was a Baptist minister. The Reverend
Nemiah Collins and his wife, Mary, were forced to quit school and go
to work so early that neither went beyond eighth grade. But their lack
of formal education certainly didn't hinder them from turning out a
son with a steely character and high intelligence. That the Reverend
Mr. Collins and Mrs. Collins succeeded so admirably is a testament to
strong genes and parental willpower far beyond the ordinary.

Al drifted through much of his integrated high school years, doing
just enough work to get by—hardly the typical profile of a future navy
officer. The real Al Collins—quick, bright, commanding—first appeared in his after-school job at a Winn-Dixie supermarket. Impressed
with his ability to deal with people and handle difficult situations, the
store's managers offered to send Al to college. The idea was that after
graduating, he would become the store's assistant manager, then move
up to manager in five years. For that time and place, it was an as-
tounding offer, and it made Al suddenly give some thought to his future. Characteristically, he looked at the deal from all sides—and

concluded that the Winn-Dixie offer might be a nine-year trip to not much. Al had bigger dreams.

Al was more taken with one of his neighbors who had joined the navy. The sailor came home in his dress whites and rakish cap, impressing the girls with his tall tales of high life at sea and the boys with stories of his low life in strange ports with exotic names. Al was intrigued. So he paid a call on the local navy recruiter, who said he could be off to boot camp by the end of the week.

His mother took him to the bus that would carry him to boot camp in Orlando, Florida, and her parting words were memorable: "Look, son, the only thing I can tell you is this: you'll never be a great leader until you're a great follower. These navy people know what they're doing, so do what they tell you, and you'll be fine."

I wish Al's mother had convoyed me to the U.S. Naval Academy with the same sailing orders, which I eventually learned for myself—the hard way. Actually, my parents were stunned to hear that the academy had commandeered one of their seven children. Most of my family had gone to Penn State, and they assumed I would too. Barring that, they couldn't understand why I'd chosen Annapolis while turning down offers to play football for Duke University or the College of William and Mary. Once they got over their initial shock, though, Mom lavished me with hugs and kisses, and Dad gave earnest advice about character and values. Sweet stuff, for sure, but not quite the practical wisdom offered by Mrs. Collins.

Being a great follower isn't just about keeping your head down and obeying orders. It means learning to understand the system from the keel up. Sure you have to acquire leadership skills so you can motivate people, but extraordinary results will elude you unless and until you develop technical expertise in your field.

I remembered that lesson when I began to assess my personnel needs as commanding officer of *Benfold*. Newly arriving division officers had two main jobs: One was to take care of the paperwork and administration of their division. The other was to become a war fighter and a watch stander in the engineering department, the combat information center, or on the bridge. I didn't concern myself with the paper pushing. That would get done one way or another—and even if it didn't, it wouldn't sink my ship. What I needed were war fighters and watch standers.

So when new officers came aboard, I didn't give them a division of people to lead. I gave them four-month assignments to learn everything there was to know about one or another watch station, whether it was antisubmarine warfare coordinator, or engineering officer of the watch, or antiair warfare coordinator. Their performance showed me what they were made of, what kind of followers they were, and how well they fit aboard ship.

Al Collins must have put his mom's advice to work immediately. From the moment they handed him a recruit's baggy uniform in Orlando, he performed brilliantly. When his parents came for his graduation, the commander took them aside and said, "It's rare we have guys who catch on as quickly as he does and are so disciplined." Al told me he hadn't done anything spectacular: "I was just either smart enough or dumb enough to do what I was told and find out how things worked." He kept doing that, and it kept working.

Years later, when Al was commanding USS *Gladiator*, a mine countermeasure ship, the same principle served him well. The ship was due for its periodic engineering inspection, a five-day ordeal (I should know) mercifully called OPPE instead of its full moniker, operational propulsion plan examination. By then, Al was a technology whiz, but he was no engineer. However, the navy provides checklists and guidelines for passing the test, and lacking any other plan, Al told his crew just to follow the book to the letter. It took them four months to get ready for the test, meticulously replacing every worn part, correcting unsanctioned procedures, and putting every tool and spare piece of equipment in its ordained place.

The inspectors came aboard and did hundreds of tests, both at anchor and under way, for three days. Then Al was told to take the ship home, two days ahead of schedule. *Gladiator* got the highest score in the history of its vessel class, eleven "excellents" for management programs out of a possible thirteen. The navy promptly flew Al to a special cram school for prospective skippers to lecture them on how to pass the dreaded OPPE. "It's simple," he told them, mimicking his mother's advice from that long-ago day when he was just setting off on his military career. "The navy has given you all the answers. Success is built into the programs. If you just believe that and do what you're told, you're home free. It's all about doing what you're told."

That great leaders must first be great followers is a lesson with a corollary: Leaders and organizations must enable followers. The goals they set must be so clear and realistic that they make performance a breeze. That's what the navy did for Al Collins and his crew aboard *Gladiator.*

That's also what Al meant when he told me that a good leader "builds success into the system." That doesn't mean doing away with hurdles and standards. It does mean specifying what is expected and helping your people master it fast and early.

Assigned to shore duty one year, Al found himself in San Diego testing computer software at something called NTISA (Navy Tactical Interoperability Support Activity). That's navy gobbledygook for a crucial operation: making sure all the navy's electronic combat systems not only work but mesh seamlessly, without the gremlins that could conceivably throw whole fleets into chaos. Al had no direct experience in testing software, but he had done development work for the navy at Sperry Rand that gave him an edge in electronics. So within months he was the navy's leading test director for tactical data systems digital-data links. He spent three years traveling to software development companies around the country, making sure their new programs actually worked and were compatible with the navy's systems as a whole. In the process, he learned a lot about programming and data systems in general.

Al also pulled off another coup: he cut in half the average time it took to certify a new software program as combat ready. His trick, simple and seemingly obvious, was to give his team of developers the navy's tests in advance so they would know what standards their programs had to meet.

Traditionally, the navy is as secretive as a high school geometry teacher in guarding its tests. But for the life of him, Al couldn't figure out why. What the navy needed were war-fighting programs that met its rigid standards. As long as the software did that, who cared how the developers achieved it? If they could find problems and correct them before Al showed up, so much the better, he reasoned. Under the old system, getting programs certified was taking months and sometimes years. Al could expedite the process because he was, in his own words, "only interested in getting good products to the fleet, so the sailors could exchange data."

The whole experience just reinforced Al's conviction that a good leader succeeds by building success into the system, by making sure everyone knows what success looks like and has the tools needed to achieve it—in this case, the formerly top-secret navy standards for software programs. "The bottom line is that people's lives depended on what we were doing out there," he told me. "The more everyone knows, the better off we are as a whole."

Indeed, secrecy is often the enemy of security. When only a few mandarins know what's really important, there is far more chance of misjudgment than when lots of eyes, ears, and minds can pool their perceptions and proposed solutions. If prospective leaders must learn to follow, their organizations must first make that possible.

Sometimes I think Al should create a worldwide best seller: *The Collins Encyclopedia of Surefire Leadership in Any Situation.* He is living proof of the notion that dedicated, resourceful leaders within large organizations can forge their own independent paths to success. He says I think too much. What I've done instead is to collect some of his most insightful lessons and lay them out for you in this chapter. Here goes:

LESSON: Be realistic, not reckless.

Jumping to conclusions is a bad enough habit in civilian life; in the military, particularly in war or any other dangerous situation, it can literally be fatal. I always knew this in theory, but Al Collins made me a true believer at 0430 on August 2, 1990. We were young officers aboard USS *England,* an old cruiser equipped with long-range guided missiles that was helping to contain Saddam Hussein's machinations in the Persian Gulf. We didn't know it at the time, but Saddam was invading Kuwait. As combat systems officer, I was galvanized by radar reports of twenty-one fighter planes streaking our way. We nervously prepared to fire the first salvo of missiles. The captain was just about to order "Batteries released!" when Al shouted, "Check fire! Check fire! Wait! Not yet!"

My pulse was beating at what felt like four hundred beats per minute. I will never forget the feeling. The captain was breathing down my neck. I didn't see what Al was seeing, but I had never known him to be wrong. The pressure was excruciating.

At eighty-two miles away, Al detected fighters making a right turn toward Saudi Arabia. Hours later, navy intelligence informed us that the planes were the fleeing Kuwaiti air force. Had we shot them down—jumping to my own conclusion and ignoring Al's far smarter reaction—well, I don't even want to imagine the result in needless loss of Kuwaiti lives, U.S. taxpayer dollars, and the navy's reputation, not to mention the certain end of my career.

Great soldiers are invariably aggressive, but the reckless ones rarely survive long enough to win skirmishes, let alone wars. The Civil War was full of impetuous cavalrymen. George Custer, a wild and woolly Union major general at twenty-six, was fated to die at thirty-seven in Montana, where he misled more than 260 soldiers to extinction against an Indian force ten times bigger than his. General Jeb Stuart, the brilliant Confederate raider, favored gold spurs, scarlet cloaks, ostrich-feathered hats, and lots of beautiful women. His boldness as Robert E. Lee's chief scout was crucial to Confederate successes early in the war. But during the battle of Gettysburg, his grandstanding left Lee vulnerable to defeat and Stuart to disgrace. He died in battle at thirty-one.

My take on modern warfare is that we can't afford swashbucklers. When they take show-offy risks, they do the enemy's work, endangering the good guys more than the bad. All organizations need leaders who confront tough situations with self-confidence tempered by caution and self-preservation. We need realists, not exhibitionists.

Stay realistic at all times—that's the underlying theme of the Al Collins story. From green recruit to commander of his own ship, Al's navy career progressed at a dazzling pace. While rising through the ranks, he gathered mentors and patrons, became an officer, and took a leading role in a historic, multidimensional cruise aboard USS *Truxtun* as part of the carrier USS *Enterprise*'s battle group. As the ships were headed for shore leave in Australia, one of the most welcoming places in the world for U.S. sailors, the battle group commander decided that each ship could send one officer ahead as liaison to arrange details of the port visit. Since that lucky officer would get four extra days in Australia, everyone wanted the plum. So *Truxtun*'s executive officer turned it into a popularity contest. After a one-day campaign, the liaison would be elected by a vote of the whole crew.

Al Collins won the vote.

"I went around the ship promising all sorts of things," he laughingly recalled, "shining people's shoes, delivering them coffee in the morning." It was a far cry from his arrival on the ship, when he had been pegged as a cocky hotshot because of his rapid rise and astonishing achievements. But afterward, Al had made himself generally popular with both officers and sailors—and he was also getting credit for the way he handled antiair warfare commander duties for the battle group, a performance that brought kudos for everyone aboard the ship.

The elected liaisons began the trip by assembling on the carrier for dinner at the admiral's table, where the conversation was lively. At one point, it touched on the comparative safety of various types of planes, and the consensus was that the S-3 Viking had a fairly ugly safety record, while C-2s were as safe as sitting at home on your living room sofa. So when the group met again at dawn on the flight deck and saw an S-3 and a C-2 waiting to take them to Australia, Al headed straight for the C-2. He liked the odds.

About halfway through the four-hour flight, the dozing passengers in the windowless tube were jolted awake by a thunderous explosion. The plane shuddered and nosed down, both engines dead. Al's fellow passengers, most of them pilots, were white with terror. The air crewman came through the cabin, pulling insulation from the walls to determine what had happened. Finally, he ripped away a panel and saw daylight. The propeller of the port-side engine had simply spun off, slicing a gash down the side of the fuselage.

Miraculously, the pilot managed to air start the starboard engine and pull the plane out of its nosedive. The ill-fated C-2 limped into Australia, but it had to be scrapped. When Al asked the pilot how close they had come to disaster, all he would say was, "You really don't want to know." Downing a stiff drink as he told me the story, Al reflected: "Well, so much for the odds. They tell you which risk is heavier and which is lighter, but they don't make you safe. Danger is always there, and you always have to expect it."

Knowing the odds is important, but only you can win the battle, and you do that by using your head. For successful leaders, caution and courage are two sides of the same winning coin.

LESSON: Bide your time, and time your beefs.

It's not always easy to keep your cool when you're one lone sailor on a big ship and you start to feel either invisible or mistreated. I can't begin to remember all the times I was enraged by some perceived idiocy or injustice during my years in the navy—and I was a rising officer with some clout. Even so, few squeaky wheels of any size get greased in a big organization that values discipline infinitely more than dissent. Still, I'm not the type to suffer in silence. I speak up, but I make sure to couch my challenge (respectfully, of course) to superiors in terms of helping the organization, not just myself. And early in my career, I quickly learned the wisdom of firing my volley only at the most opportune moment, giving it my best shot, and then if it didn't work, shutting up.

Al Collins seemed to know instinctively how to time his beefs—

even when he first reported as an apprentice seaman on USS *Lexington,* an aircraft carrier with a crew of two thousand based in Pensacola, Florida. In those days, racial integration was still evolving in a navy that had been segregated for nearly two centuries. A few African Americans had become junior officers or enlisted specialists in hot fields like communications and electronics. Far more were cooks. Navy ships still had stewards, mostly blacks and Filipinos, who performed valet services for the officers aboard.

Navy tradition calls for new recruits to spend their first three months at sea as mess attendants, peeling potatoes, washing dishes for the cooks, and cleaning up after people. I can tell you that mess duty sucks. The rest of the crew makes fun of you, and it can be tough. But it's a rite of passage that every recruit has to go through.

Al cheerfully went to work, expecting to move on to equally menial chores on deck—chipping away old paint and recoating with new or loading stores—while he learned a more complex duty. He told me he wanted to be an electronics technician, but the recruiter had said he wasn't "smart enough" for that. (Al later became branch chief for cyberwarfare on the very smart staff of the Joint Chiefs at the Pentagon during the Iraq war.) There was one African American sailor in the radar division, and Al got to know him.

Ninety days came and went, and other rookies moved on to deck duty. But Al was still scrubbing pots. He began to suspect that he was being classed by the color of his skin, but he didn't complain. Since he was blessed with talent and a winning personality, some of his shipmates rallied to his cause. "Man, they're screwing you," said one of the white cooks with whom he had become friendly. "You need to go straight to the captain." Then the cook offered a shrewd assessment: "If you put in a formal request, they'll try to persuade you not to; when you ask to see the captain, people will do whatever you want to keep you from making trouble." Every sailor in the U.S. Navy has the right to submit a special request chit to see the commanding officer if he or she perceives unjust treatment. And if the sailor is correct, the chain of command will usually try to placate the sailor in order to avoid being embarrassed in front of the captain.

As always, Al knew good advice when he heard it, and sure enough, when his request landed like a hot rivet on the desk of the supply officer who ran the galley, the officer summoned Al and asked what he wanted. No problem, the supply officer said. If Al would withdraw his request to speak directly to the captain, the officer would put Al in any division he wanted aboard ship. Al checked with his friend in radar. That afternoon Al was in radar too. By waiting until the time was right to speak up, he had bypassed months of chipping paint on deck, and he had learned another lesson about making his own way within the navy's mammoth bureaucracy.

LESSON: When you need help, reach out.

After several rapid promotions, Al Collins reported aboard USS *San Bernardino* as the senior petty officer in the Operation Intelligence (OI) Division. The ship was a tank landing craft designed to ground on a beach and open its clamshell bows to disembark a marine invasion force. Though Al had more seniority than the other enlisted men, he knew nothing about the mission or operating such a vessel. That can sometimes happen in the navy as you progress through the ranks. You keep taking on greater responsibility until, one day, you find yourself at a more senior level and expected to do a job you know little if anything about.

An amphibious ship's sole purpose in life is to carry marines from their U.S. and Japanese bases to wherever the scene of action is and put them ashore. It's the navy's responsibility to get them ashore safely. It requires a special set of both technical and leadership skills. "It was all Greek to me," Al told me. "It's not in the mainstream of what people do on warships." He planned to learn what he needed to know from his two junior petty officers, but luck ran against him. Soon after he came aboard, *San Bernardino* was assigned to lead a major exercise with five other ships delivering marines to a beach in choreographed sequence at just the right moment. Al, who had never even seen such an exercise, was responsible for coordinating all five vessels by radio, and controlling their marine-filled landing crafts to the beach. He had never handled a radio before, and this was his first post with people reporting to him. Having always taken orders, he now had to give them.

"It was bloody," he admitted. The navy inspector announced that he had never seen a worse performance. And even though the exercise was to be run again in two days, the inspector basically wrote Al off: "I don't think you can ever do this," he told him.

The captain could have given the job to someone else, but he didn't. Instead, he asked whether Al had a plan. Well, not really, but he did have shipmates. Al called his men together and asked for their help. They agreed that the odds were against them, but they were willing to try to teach him enough to coordinate the exercise.

"They were good guys, and we were all young," Al explained. The men hadn't much liked his predecessor, but Al had already won their respect by admitting outright that he knew nothing about the job and wanted to learn. No bluster. No baloney. No blaming the person who scheduled the exercise before Al could get up to speed. It was his frankness, humility, and enthusiasm that got him through the next two days. And when the exercise was run again, "it wasn't a stellar performance," he said, "but we got the marines ashore on time."

Al stayed on *San Bernardino* for three years and did so well that before he left, the captain singled him out of a crew of two hundred for what's called a command advancement, a promotion without competing against his peers or taking a test. A commanding officer can meritoriously promote three superbly performing sailors each year.

Al was slow to appreciate the value of formal education; three times in his early floundering he had passed up chances to go to school. But he always found mentors who recognized what he was worth, and they pushed him—sometimes against his will—to live up to his promise. When he finally caught on to the value of "book learning," he signed up for off-duty classes wherever he was stationed. So now Al's alma maters include the University of South Alabama, National University in Washington, D.C., and the University of California, San Diego.

But that's not the whole story. I don't have to tell you that Al was a bright young sailor willing to learn anything from anyone. One of the characteristics that lifted him above other bright young sailors, though, was the way he inspired people to want to teach him. Because he admitted ignorance, threw himself on their mercy, and made them feel good in sharing their knowledge, his shipmates couldn't resist. He made them feel like heroes. Al's satisfying response made teaching him a group pleasure, which, in turn, boosted group competence.

Knowledge seeking, it turns out, is contagious. To train a whole crew, you may need only one dynamic seeker like Al Collins to spark a teamwide pursuit of learning.

LESSON: Command with compassion.

Al learned the power of compassionate command as a petty officer aboard USS *Pegasus,* the navy's first hydrofoil, based in Key West, Florida. This high-tech vessel was designed to virtually fly over the water on its struts and foils at more than forty-three knots while firing cruise missiles at enemy squadrons. Al landed a spot on *Pegasus* after his performance caught a captain's eye (and not for the first time, I can guarantee you). Al's previous ship had been escorting *Pegasus* when one of the hydrofoil's sailors got sick and had to be flown ashore. Sent to fill in, Al got an invitation to stay when the skipper saw how quickly he mastered new skills.

Shortly after that, Al took shore leave in Key West to be with his wife, Billie, who was about to deliver their second child. But just before the birth, Captain Jim Orvis called to ask Al to come back immediately for a trip to Puerto Rico to test the hydrofoil's cruise missiles. It was Al who worked out the plan for actually firing the missiles, which the captain had never done, and Al who got the credit when they scored direct hits. No doubt pleased with Al's performance and aware of what he had sacrificed to make the captain and his ship look good,

Orvis flew Al home at navy expense to be with his wife and new son for as long as it took to get acquainted.

A year later, the boy came down with an apparent cold that hung on. The navy doctors at the base hospital in Key West said not to worry, but when the baby seemed to get sicker, Al told Billie to take him to a civilian hospital. There doctors diagnosed double pneumonia and had the baby flown to specialists in Miami in time to save his life. Captain Orvis told Al just to go, to be with his family. It was a month before Al reported for duty again, but Orvis didn't even charge it against his leave time.

Years later, when Al was skipper of his own ship, the wife of his key engineer, Chief Petty Officer Tom Carney, contracted a mysterious illness. Al told Carney to go home and stay with her. The illness brought on paralysis, and when Carney came aboard ship three months later, he was resigned to the fact that his wife wasn't going to get better. Understanding that Carney needed a shore job so he could look after her, Al unhesitatingly arranged a transfer.

Carney was a top-notch engineer whom Al never managed to replace. The ship suffered without his skills and experience. "Chief Carney was the best we had to offer," Al told me. "If I had a question about the engineering, he was the guy. That was a very, very significant loss." If the country had been at war, Al couldn't have let him go. But it was peacetime, and Al believed that a good man shouldn't be made to suffer more than he had to.

Carney returned for a visit and tearfully told Al that this was the way the navy should work, but he had never seen it happen before. Don't worry about it, Al said. "Just do the same for someone else."

Compassion is a powerful leadership tool that engages people emotionally. By sympathizing with someone in pain or trouble, actively reaching out to help, and making a difference, a leader can trigger a deep-seated response amounting to "I'll follow you anywhere." What is more, a person receiving compassion is apt, like Al Collins, to become a proselytizer for doing the right thing when a teammate is in trouble. And the more your people help each other in tough times, the stronger your organization becomes.

LESSON: Seize the day, and help others do the same.

The military's need for top talent in all ranks is a life-and-death priority. Accordingly, the armed services work harder at developing talent than many civilian organizations. For one thing, they regularly rank every officer's fitness, promote those who improve, and ease out those who don't deserve promotion. It's a tough system, not always fair but generally able to separate the best from the rest. In these circumstances, it becomes every officer's duty to identify talented people, challenge them to grow, and push them upward. This very definitely includes the most junior enlisted personnel. These young men and women often join today's all-volunteer military in search of a free college education, and their drive and determination tend to make them considerably more educable than some of their predecessors.

When Al Collins enlisted in the navy more than three decades ago, he didn't yet know the value of education, but he came to exemplify sailors who use the navy as an opportunity machine, to the navy's benefit as well as their own.

A year before he came aboard *Pegasus,* the hydrofoil had literally run aground, doing considerable damage to its delicate undercarriage. The problem? Its sheer speed. *Pegasus,* as I mentioned earlier, was the fastest ship in the navy, designed to skim the water at about forty-three knots (nearly fifty miles per hour), and the navy's navigation systems simply couldn't track the charts at that speed. However, the Sperry Rand Corporation was developing something called a High-Speed Collision Avoidance Navigation System, so Captain Orvis sent Al to Sperry's labs in Reston, Virginia, to help adapt it for use in a hydrofoil. Al participated in the engineering development for several months and learned the system inside out.

When he took the system back to *Pegasus,* Al was the only man aboard the small ship (five officers, seventeen enlisted sailors) who knew how to work it. It fell to Al, an enlisted man, to teach the officers how to run their ship. In the old navy, that would have been an awkward situation for the officers. But *Pegasus* was a bit like a high-tech start-up: Cutting-edge learning created excitement, and respect was earned by brains, not rank.

Al's lack of formal education certainly didn't bother Orvis or Andy Singer, his combat systems officer, and the other officers were young enough not to resent him. Watching Al's performance, Orvis had a growing admiration and respect for his abilities. But the skipper was concerned with the thought of great talent going to waste, and he considered it his duty to take command of Al's bright future and accelerate its progress. As the captain saw it, running a ship meant more, much more, than just barking orders. Orvis "pushed me all along," Al told me. "He wanted me to realize my full potential and go as far as I wanted to go. Once he said, 'Collins, if you don't put in an application for this officer's program, I'm going to kick your ass.'"

After mastering and teaching the navigation system, Al seized an opportunity to move on to tactics and strategy. Working with Singer, he developed exercise plans and refined them with the captain. The ship's crew played several simulated battle games in which *Pegasus* challenged aircraft carrier battle groups, lurking undetected until the ships came within range and then firing cruise missiles to sink the carrier.

Al's role was crucial: he became de facto operations officer of *Pegasus* and carefully planned the ship's movements for approval by the captain. Lying quietly in wait with all transmitting equipment shut down, the hydrofoil would listen for electronic emissions from the battle group—not just radar signals, but virtually anything in the electromagnetic spectrum, including radio transmissions and the signal waves generated by running engines. Al would triangulate the source and calculate where to aim the missiles. In the simulated firing, a radar ping would signal each of five missiles headed for the carrier in Al's sights. Referees on the carrier later verified that when they heard the pings, the ship was at the precise spot Al had targeted. "One hundred percent of the time, we were successful in getting in, attacking, and then sprinting out of there before they knew what hit them," Al told me.

Shortly before Al's *Pegasus* tour ended, he followed Orvis's advice and applied to be commissioned as an officer. As I mentioned before, there are other ways of becoming an officer in the navy besides going to the Naval Academy as I did. You can go to ROTC or OCS and get commissioned as an ensign once you successfully complete the curriculum. That is how we get probably 85 percent of our officers in the navy. But there is another way to become an officer without having a college degree. If you are a senior petty officer who demonstrates outstanding technical capability and leadership skills, you can apply to become a limited duty officer. That is what Al did. At the same time, he took the test for promotion to chief petty officer. He qualified for both. Al had been an acting officer for a long time, but he went to his next berth on USS *Truxtun* as an ensign, the real thing.

Because Captain Orvis had been committed to making Al Collins live up to his promise, an enlisted-man-turned-officer went on to carve out an impressive career path within the navy's bureaucracy.

LESSON: Show off when you have to.

The navy, like the other U.S. military services, is a meritocracy. But I can hardly claim that military people live and work in an ego-free zone, devoid of the envy, jealousy, and resentment that commonly afflict humankind, no matter how noble we military personnel are (or think we are). The problem turns on how to manage those emotions without becoming victims or villains. What it comes down to is accountability—but not in the way you may think. Just as it is important to admit your mistakes, it's equally important to acknowledge your strengths—not with smart-ass bragging, but with quiet confidence. As Al Collins discovered during his service on *Truxtun,* owning up to your prodigious talents may be the only way to turn jealousy and resentment into honest admiration and respect.

In the easygoing democracy of *Pegasus,* Al's assignment before he boarded *Truxtun,* his status as an enlisted man with an officer's portfolio hadn't been a problem. Ironically, when he arrived on *Truxtun* as a newly commissioned ensign, he found himself deeply resented.

Truxtun was a nuclear-powered guided missile cruiser, one of the navy's newest and most prestigious ships. It had a crew of five hundred with fifty officers, nearly all of them senior to Al. Most of the officers had also been through nuclear engineering training, which is excruciating. Only the smartest get admitted, and not all survive the rigorous academic requirements. Many of those who do survive develop a certain intellectual arrogance toward those who didn't go through it.

But of the fifty officers on *Truxtun,* only five could lay claim to being a Surface Warfare Qualified Officer, and without it, they couldn't get promoted. Getting this designation is a huge deal and requires an arduous qualification process. Once you qualify, you get to wear a gold pin above your left breast pocket, signifying that you have passed muster. Al had passed the qualification on *Pegasus* and got to wear the pin after getting commissioned. So the *Truxtun* officers, who considered themselves intellectually superior by virtue of their nuclear engineering training, greeted the newly fledged ensign with his SWO pin as a hotshot due a certain respect, but not much. In truth, they were jealous.

At training sessions in the wardroom, Challenge Al became a favorite game. Whenever a hard question came up, someone would say sarcastically, "Let Collins answer it; he's surface warfare qualified." Knowing Al, I wasn't surprised to learn that he always had the right answer. But after the game had gone on for a while, Al decided to hit back. He issued his own challenge: "Okay, guys, here's the deal. Pick any subject in surface warfare and put together any ten questions on it. I'll go head to head on them with any officer on this ship except the skipper, and I guarantee I'll come out on top."

There was a sudden silence. A few of his shipmates glared at him, some exchanged amused glances, and others studied their shoes. None accepted the challenge.

Problem solved. "From that day forward," Al told me, "I didn't have any more trouble or any more issues."

He did, however, get a call from the executive officer, who commented on Al's gutsy response and offered to help if there were any more snide remarks. There weren't. Instead, people started asking him serious questions about problems they couldn't solve, and Al added to his wide circle of friends by lending a helping hand.

I got a chance to do a little legitimate showing-off myself in the Iran crisis of 1997 when the *Nimitz* battle group entered the Persian Gulf and anchored off Bahrain for strategic briefings.

While the carrier and its cruisers were at anchor, *Benfold,* which had arrived ten days earlier, was given responsibility for the air defense of the battle group. We spotted an Iranian patrol craft, a P-3, approaching the battle group to perform surveillance. As you might imagine, the navy is not keen on letting foreign aircraft fly too close to its carriers. For one thing, there's nothing to keep a plane from diving into a ship and destroying it. The P-3 had to be contacted on the international air distress frequency and told to stand clear.

USS *Lake Champlain,* which happened to be commanded by the most senior captain in the Pacific fleet, was the ship in the best position to send that signal. It was my job, as commander of *Benfold,* to give the order to contact the P-3. And that's how it happened that the most junior captain in the fleet, me, got to give an order to the most senior captain—an irony noted by every naval officer in the entire Persian Gulf.

The Iranian aircraft was successfully contacted and flew away. But I later heard that the CO of *Champlain* was not happy about being ordered around by an underling. Who could blame him? Even though I was only doing my job, he might have seen it as showboating. Another captain more wrapped up in rank might have been so miffed as to delay or even resist my order, and that could have led to disaster. To the credit of the *Lake Champlain's* CO, nothing like that happened.

LESSON: Make yourself a learning machine.

In the navy, as elsewhere, I've often heard that old chestnut, "It's not what you know, it's who you know." Maybe so. But there's a hard core of spectacular achievers like Al Collins who put the lie to such cynicism. How else to explain why the U.S. Navy can boast the best crews sailing the finest warships on the seven seas?

Al's cruiser *Truxtun* was one of the prime ships in the battle group screening the aircraft carrier USS *Enterprise*. As such, *Truxtun* drew the prestigious job of the battle group's antiair warfare commander, defending against anything that flew—from airplanes to cruise missiles—and controlling and coordinating all the group's own warplanes. It was a three-dimensional chess game at supersonic speed, and a far bigger picture than most people ever look at. The only problem was that no one on *Truxtun* had ever done it. Perhaps inevitably, Al Collins was handed the assignment and challenged to make good on it.

Al immediately plunged into learning every relevant fact available, but that barely qualified him as an apprentice in the arcane art he had to master on behalf of an entire battle group. Nevertheless, he and *Truxtun's* operations officer cobbled together a plan and ran the group's first exercise. It wasn't quite the fiasco of the landing-craft practice on *San Bernardino,* but it was sorry enough to earn Al an invitation to take a crash course in running the carrier's planes without destroying them.

The "crash course" turned into a two-month training program—the equivalent of a high-speed master's degree in antiair warfare. Al also flew as a passenger in every model of plane aboard the carrier so he could gauge its abilities and limitations when he was in control. He returned to *Truxtun* knowing the job forward and backward.

That was in 1986, just after *Truxtun* joined the *Enterprise* battle group and set sail on what had been planned as a routine cruise of the western Pacific. It turned out to be a short course in the geopolitical big picture of the mid-1980s. First, the group was sent to provide air cover to forestall a military coup against Corazon Aquino's new government in the Philippines. Next, it skipped across the Indian Ocean to the Arabian Sea to protect the plane carrying Vice President George H. W. Bush (he was on a Middle East trip, and the Iranians had threatened to shoot him down). After that, the carrier group's western Pacific cruise veered through the Suez Canal to the Mediterranean, where *Enterprise* joined two other carriers cruising off the coast of Libya during one of the periodic crises provoked by its dictator, Muammar Qaddafi. When Libya fired missiles at U.S. warplanes, the three-carrier group retaliated by sinking two Libyan ships and bombing a missile site.

It was Al who developed and ran the air-defense plan in the Philippines, and it was his plan that set up a safe corridor past the coast of Iran for the vice president's plane. Off the Libyan coast, the group rotated responsibility for air defense, so at times Al was not just looking at the big picture, he was running it—controlling all the planes from three carriers. He was still an ensign, the lowest officer rating in the navy, but he was a learning—and I might add performing—machine.

Throughout Al Collins's career, it was his unflagging pursuit of intellectual challenges—not of powerful superiors—that made him a star of the modern navy.

LESSON: Figure out what's important, and act on it.

When a crowd faces a sudden emergency, several people may eagerly propose remedies, but typically, just one person will offer an idea that makes sense. That's a leader, a person who finds solutions that work. That singular ability to see the best way onward and upward is precisely what attracts followers.

I'm sure Al Collins was born with this unique ability, but he probably had no idea how instinctive it was back when we were both stationed at the navy base in San Diego. At the time, he was testing software and I was the executive officer of USS *Shiloh*. Al, who had risen all the way from seaman to the rank of lieutenant commander by then, was thinking he might be nearing the end of his navy career. The rule is Up or out—if you don't get promoted every few years, you resign or retire. He could have finished his career as the executive officer on a good ship. But his rank also meant he could apply for command of a ship. I pushed him to go for it. He did, and he was selected.

Anyone taking command of a ship has to go to Prospective Commanding Officer (PCO) school. Even if you're a veteran, you always go back for this refresher course when you get a new ship. It's a comprehensive class on all the navy dos and don'ts: principles of command, techniques of leadership, what to report and when to report it—everything required to be a skipper. Candidates attend seminars with visiting VIPs, including admirals, former commanding officers, other navy brass, and anyone else who can give sound advice on how to stay out of trouble.

The piece of advice Al remembers best came from an admiral. His words of wisdom? Simply this: there's absolutely no way to make sure you get everything right. This sage, whose name Al says he's forgotten but whose words still resonate, said the navy issues endless orders, rules, notices, instructions, and guidelines. That's fine, the admiral said, but there's no way you can comply with all of them in your two years of command. You can't do it; it's impossible. "Your job," he went on, "is to figure out what's important, and act on it. Period. That's it."

The light went on, Al said, and from then on he considered most of the school's other lessons as secondary to this guiding principle. Al's first question in nearly every new situation throughout the rest of his career was: What's really important here?

Al's first command was USS *Gladiator,* a mine countermeasure ship, or what the shorthand-crazy navy calls an MCM. Once called minesweepers, these ships have become so high tech that the label is outdated. *Gladiator,* for instance, is built of wood covered with fiberglass and powered by aluminum engines to prevent it from giving off an electromagnetic signal that could trigger a sophisticated mine. Trained dolphins are used to locate mines and clip their moorings or leave packages of explosives to blow them up. The ship also has two tethered robots that can be sent to incapacitate very deep mines designed to kill submarines.

Gladiator was on a Mediterranean tour when Al took command in Lisbon. Within days, it was time to test the robots. Like something out of a teenage techie's dream, these expensive, sophisticated weapons are equipped with their own sonar devices, bomb bays to carry explosives, and fore and aft cameras feeding live video pictures up the umbilical to the specialists who control the bots with a joystick. But the robots are by no means trouble free, and to deploy them risked damaging or losing them. Carefully, the operators got one of the robots into the water, sent it out perhaps three hundred yards or so, and then said it was time to retrieve it.

Al, watching from the ship's command center, said, "Wait a minute. Retrieve it? Why? How far will it go?"

"Fifteen hundred yards, sir."

"Then let's do that. Let it out."

They looked at each other nervously. "Sir, we've never done that." They explained that they had been taught that the risk of damage was too great.

Al was caught in a dilemma. On the one hand, there was little justification in peacetime for risking either equipment or life and limb. But on the other, if the machines were ever needed for serious work, he and the crew had to know what they could actually do.

Too often in civilian life and the military, leaders are afraid to push the envelope; they shy away because they fear failure. It's easier to play it safe and leave the risk taking to someone else. The catch is that eventually their companies founder and their careers go bust because, as any successful investor will tell you, you have to take some prudent and calculated risk to gain your reward.

So Al, remembering the admiral's advice, asked himself: what is the ultimate goal here? He didn't need to think for long: the reason we're here is to provide a frontline defense for the nation.

"If I'm going to use this thing to perform this function, we have to practice doing it," he told the crew. "If it breaks, it breaks. I'd rather it break now than when it's really needed."

So the operators reeled the robot deep into the ocean, where it promptly malfunctioned. In theory, if something broke down, the robot was designed to sever the umbilical and return to the surface. It did bob up out of the water but with its tether still attached, so there had been at least two failures.

Later, Al called the supply house and ordered the parts to repair the robot. But he also called the designers and told them their equipment wasn't performing to specifications and they needed to redesign it. Because he had been able to shrug off the distractions and home in on the real reason for running the robot test, he had gained critical knowledge about the limits of his equipment, knowledge that couldn't have been gotten any other way. Furthermore, *Gladiator*'s crew had a much better idea of what their new skipper expected of them and the ship.

Like Al with the sailors operating *Gladiator*'s robot, I pushed the gunner's mates on *Benfold* to make sure we were combat ready at all times.

As a destroyer, *Benfold* had a single five-inch gun that fired fifty-pound bullets. Designed to take out enemy missiles, ships, and aircraft or to support a beach landing, the gun has to be fired regularly or it will break down. (It has hydraulic seals that can dry up and crack if the gun isn't used, dripping oil and hydraulic fluid all over the place.) The only way to keep it operating properly is to constantly stress it. The navy lays down training requirements, including regular gunnery exercises, in which a ship and its crew are graded and given readiness ratings. But budget constraints limiting our allotment of bullets for training made it virtually impossible to achieve excellence. We would get maybe fifty bullets to shoot each quarter. Part of my job as commander of *Benfold*, however, was to achieve excellence. Where there's a will, there's a way—in this case, the U.S. Marine Corps.

The marines have their own requirements for training spotters, the people who radio a ship's gunners and help them guide the bullets to the target. And to accomplish their training, they also have their own huge allotment of bullets that navy ships can use. Lucky for us, the marines trained their spotters on the same firing range *Benfold* used. So the key was to volunteer to provide spotting practice for the marines, using their bullets, and then we would all have a shot at achieving excellence. We achieved the feat by routinely emptying our five-hundred-bullet ammunition magazine in practice with the marines.

There was a downside with the five-inch gun, however. A bolt on the gun is susceptible to metal fatigue and can shear off after 350 or 400 firings. The gunner's mates liked to fire the five-incher, but they weren't happy when I insisted that we empty our 600-bullet magazine at each practice. They didn't want to risk having the gun fail in mid-session.

I wasn't just flexing the gun to find out how long it could fire before breaking down; I was also flexing the gunner's mates. I wanted them to develop such a feel for the gun that they could anticipate a breakdown and replace the bolt just before it happened. It made more work for the crew, but in the long run, *Benfold* had a better, more reliable weapon system.

LESSON: Make a contract with your people, and honor it.

When Al took command of a new ship or whenever new crew members joined his ship, he held an orientation session to spell out his rules and expectations and the contract he was making with each sailor.

"I'm the commanding officer," Al said, "and it's the best job on the ship. I wake up nearly every morning feeling pretty good about it. But it's not all fun, and some days I get up feeling downright lousy. So I don't expect you to jump out of bed and do somersaults every morning because you're so glad to be here. But I do expect you to be pretty satisfied with your lot here and your work environment, and to feel that you're getting what you expected out of this assignment.

"Here's the contract we make," he went on: "You joined the navy for a specific reason. I don't know that reason, but I'd like to know what it is so I can help you get what you want—whether it's to learn a trade, to further your education through the G.I. Bill, or to make a career in the navy. And our part of that contract is to provide you with a good working environment; pay for your services (though not very much); good health care; a skill and a chance to use it; and if you want it and if you fit the navy's needs, a career. Now I'm here to see to it that we do our part."

But Al wasn't finished. Having come up through the ranks as an enlisted man himself, he well knew that the navy life wasn't for everyone, and young men and women, especially those with few options, might soon come to regret their choice. So he added a crucial caveat: "If you wake up in the morning and you find yourself hating what you do, then you need to come and talk to me, and we will work to change that."

Al meant every word, and his reason for inviting complaints was to let everyone on the ship know that there was always a way out. Sadly aware that some desperately unhappy sailors have committed suicide, Al said he'd "rather remove the guy from the ship than have him damage himself or a shipmate or my ship." His invitation was accepted just once, when an officer being treated for clinical depression felt free to let Al know he couldn't take the duty anymore. Al gladly arranged a transfer.

More often, Al himself had to make the hard judgment that a crew member wasn't cut out for the navy, and even harder, to deliver the blunt message that that sailor would never be allowed to drive Al's ship. It wasn't a black mark on the sailor's record, Al was careful to say, nor did it mean that he or she was a failure. Let's find something you're comfortable with, something you will enjoy doing every day, he'd say, and I'll help make it happen. Al even took an active part in the search. He still gets e-mail from people he's fired, and they actually thank him for it.

In my own skippering experience, firing people brought unexpected rewards—if I did it the right way. The person let go was relieved to be leaving a clearly inappropriate situation and grateful to me for helping arrange a timely escape, and I felt good midwifing the birth of a new and better life. But far more important than any personal satisfaction was what the crew saw when their captain sent misfits ashore: by upholding the dignity of each departing sailor, I honored my promise to protect the members of our crew who remained on board, and they reciprocated by working harder and smarter for the ship.

LESSON: Trust the crew to run the ship.

As luck would have it, one of the four engines broke down on the first ship that Al Collins skippered. *Gladiator*'s chief engineer came to Al to ask about the deadline for fixing it. "I don't do engines," Al told him. "You own that engine—it's yours. If it breaks, fix it; and do it as fast as you can and still do it right. If there's an operational reason, I'll tell you when I need it, so you'll know the degree of urgency. But I'm not going to give you any deadline."

It was tough for Al to put across the concept of the crew running the ship, especially because his predecessor had been a micromanager who always set deadlines. So Al, with a master's touch honed on his extraordinary journey from green recruit to commanding officer of his own ship, called a meeting of all the chiefs, the senior enlisted men. He told them flat out, "This is your ship, and you've got to run it." He explained that the officers sure couldn't do it—only one of the junior officers had ever been on a ship before. They were promising young men, Al assured the group, but green, and then he assigned his seasoned crew chiefs two missions: "One, to run the ship; two, to teach your junior officer how to do it." He finished by saying he was counting on them to do what he asked. And they did.

In some ways, this lesson is the most important leadership advice I can give you. There's an incalculable difference between an organization with a micromanaging leader who squashes everyone's initiative and an organization that frees people to take full responsibility for their jobs and perform to the best of their abilities. In the military, it's the difference between a unit that probably should be dismantled and one that's ready to fight and win. In business, it's the difference between a has-been company that struggles just to compete and one whose employees relish being on the cutting edge.

By accepting responsibility for running *Benfold,* some of my own crew members solved a fleetwide problem involving the launch of the then new Tomahawk cruise missiles. As you might guess, we had to be prepared to launch the Tomahawks on short notice, but the procedure being used by all the guided missile destroyers threatened the strict launching time lines. Flummoxed, the fleet commander was on the verge of telling the Pentagon that the mission was impossible to carry out as designed. That's when several of my mission planners, led by Petty Officer Darren Barton (he's now a chief petty officer, by the way), put their heads together to work out modified procedures that allowed us to meet the time lines. We passed along our solution to the commander, and it was adopted throughout the fleet.

I didn't tell the planners to come up with a solution. They simply knew that what they did was important, not just to their shipmates but to the safety and security of our country as a whole. They understood the big picture of military preparedness and wanted to do their part in the best way possible. I made sure, of course, that they got full credit for what they did. But praise from me or anyone else didn't matter; they would have done it anyway because it was the right thing to do.

Long before I took command of *Benfold,* I served eighteen months aboard the destroyer USS *Harry W. Hill.* It was a great ship with a fantastic commanding officer, but *Hill* had gained a modicum of fame (or maybe infamy) because every sailor on it could be easily spotted just before the ship got under way: a *Hill* sailor would, for sure, be carrying a gallon of spring water down the pier before setting out to sea.

On older navy ships, it was the boilers that produced a ship's water supply. They scooped in saltwater, heated it to boiling to remove impurities, and then flashed the resultant steam back to fresh water. *Harry W. Hill* had the worst boilers in the navy. We could leave port with our freshwater tanks topped off, but within an hour we'd have only 20 percent left. The chief engineer blamed the crew, claiming we took too long to shave and used too much fresh water each time. In fact, the boiler was poorly designed, but we razzed the engineer that he also had a leak and should fix it.

Fast-forward ten years to 1997. I'd been captain of *Benfold* for all of two months, and she'd been ordered to the Middle East. We were two days out of San Diego on a seven-day transit to Pearl Harbor. In our battle group was none other than *Harry W. Hill*. As you might guess, she was already out of water.

Now *Benfold* carried a prototype of a reverse-osmosis desalinization system. All we had to do was scoop up some saltwater, move it through a succession of increasingly fine membranes to remove the impurities, and shazam! We had clear, pure water. So I wasn't all that surprised when I received a call from the commodore, who was traveling on *Hill*. It's an embarrassing thing when the commodore is embarked on your ship and can't even brush his teeth. I had to feel a little sorry for *Hill*'s captain and crew.

Anyway, the commodore had been receiving regular reports about our new desalinization system. "Are you really at 100 percent freshwater?" he asked me. When I confirmed it, he reiterated what I already knew about *Hill*'s lack of water and then said, "Unless you can figure out some way to get water to *Hill*, I'm going to transfer over to *Benfold* and send *Hill* back to San Diego." The hairs on the back of my neck stood up. If the ship was forced to turn around, not only would the exercise planned for Pearl Harbor be scrapped, but I'd be booted out of my fancy captain's cabin so the commodore could have it. I'd be forced to live in a room the size of a closet. This was a big deal.

In the history of the U.S. Navy, no destroyer had ever transferred water to another destroyer—these ships weren't supposed to have the capability. I took the problem to Derek Nisco, the young officer in charge of the deck department, and his grizzled chief boatswain's mate, Scott Moede. (Moede, as you will recall, saved the day in our anchorage exercise off San Diego when the brake holding the anchor chain failed.) This was Derek's first division officer tour, but Chief Moede was an old and experienced hand. So they got their team together and, sure enough, they came up with a solution.

When I got back to the commodore, he started telling me how the job should be done. I interrupted him, saying, "Commodore, could I have a time-out?" When he agreed to listen, I said, "We've already scoped this out, and this is how we'd like to do it." He was taken aback at being interrupted, but he got over it as we briefed him on our plan.

To send over the freshwater, Derek and his team rigged up a way to suspend a hose in midair so that it didn't drag in the water and rip off the side fittings when we came alongside the *Hill*. I say "rigged up" because a destroyer doesn't typically carry the necessary equipment for this kind of maneuver. But my crew devised a rigid span wire with a trolley hooked to it to carry the hose back and forth. We had never practiced anything like this, but it came off without a hitch.

We transferred about twelve thousand gallons of freshwater from *Benfold* to *Hill*. *Benfold*'s percentage of freshwater dropped to about 30 percent, which got me to wondering about our own ability to make it to Pearl Harbor. But the next day, thanks to the desalinization system, we were back up to 100 percent.

I was proud of my crew when I heard that news of the transfer had made it back to the Pentagon. The point of my story, though, is that I had nothing to do with the solution to the transfer problem. I didn't make one suggestion. I let Derek and the sailors run the ship, and they did a damn sight better job of it than I could have.

It all goes back to freeing people to shoulder full responsibility for their jobs. In the military as well as in business, you won't get people to perform at their peak through traditional authoritarian methods. That kind of command-and-control model just doesn't work very well these days. As Al Collins told me, it's not that you can't still wield absolute power. You can. But if your officers and crew don't actually challenge you, they will, at the very least, perform sullenly and grudgingly.

It's far better to persuade people that your cause is a noble one worth buying into. That's why Al gathered *Gladiator*'s whole crew on his first day aboard and told them what he meant to do—his schedule for the ship, the awards they would win, and how they would do it. He was challenging them to be the best while also adding both interest and purpose to life on the ship. But more important, Al was making it very clear that the crew had a shared mission whose success depended on each person's accepting responsibility for his or her part. If anyone slacked off, the goal would become unreachable. Before long, shirking and sloppy work became socially unacceptable on *Gladiator;* everyone had taken responsibility. And when the ship started winning awards, everyone shared in the victory.

By that time, I was in the Pentagon, working for Defense Secretary William Perry, and I often talked with Al. I was delighted but not surprised when *Gladiator* swept every award in its command. I had long known that responsibility is one of the most powerful weapons in a leader's arsenal. Once your people acquire it and savor it, they will bear almost any hardship and pay almost any price—even risk their lives—to keep the pride and purpose responsibility gives them.

LESSON: Make sure the whole crew is on board.

Al was so successful at getting the best out of his *Gladiator* crew that his senior officers constantly called on him and his crew to perform chores at sea that other, less-competent, ships could not handle as well. That was fine with Al and most of his sailors too. But the families of his crew members soon became restive. It wasn't right, they complained, that *Gladiator* was always out to sea while other crews got to stay in home port because their ships had broken down or they weren't up to the required tasks.

They had a point, Al decided. At first, though, all he could come up with was the lame excuse that the system is bigger than any of us. That explanation satisfied virtually no one. Then he talked to me and to Admiral John Pearson, who had been Al's captain in his previous posting on *Truxtun*. Having taken Al's measure, Pearson gave him full autonomy to run *Gladiator* as he saw fit. That's when Al took a page from my book on *Benfold*. He began writing letters to the families of his crew, letting them know how their spouses, sons, and daughters were doing and praising their achievements. He also started a ship's newspaper, aimed as much at the families as the crew, recording *Gladiator's* triumphs and underlining the importance of its various missions.

The grumbling never fully stopped, but as the families began to understand the full importance of the jobs their loved ones were performing so well, and as they became better informed about the ship's activities and accomplishments, they began to take vicarious pride in its achievements. In effect, Al made them an extended part of the crew, and now they were on board too.

LESSON: Use might to make right.

Whether in business or the military, leaders should never underestimate the scope of their authority and responsibility in dealing with the outside world. And if a dispute with outsiders arises, it should be treated not as a personal fight, but as a defense of the organization and its paramount interests. If leaders can rise above their own emotions and limitations, they are more likely to stay cool and detached as they dispassionately weigh the cards they hold, and, invariably, they will prevail in their defense.

Al brilliantly applied this lesson when *Gladiator* was going into dry dock for several million dollars' worth of maintenance. At that point, MCMs had a dismal maintenance record; shipyards routinely fell weeks or months behind schedule when working on minesweepers, and huge cost overruns were routine. Both the shipyard supervisor and the navy's representative at the yard warned Al that problems might come up. No, he told them, that wasn't going to happen. He was bringing the ship in on schedule, and he was going to take it out on schedule. They looked at each other and smiled knowingly.

In general, navy officers are not trained in the art of negotiating with contractors. But on *Truxtun,* Admiral Pearson had taught Al about shipyards and how to deal with them. Pearson told him the yards played games. His blunt advice: "Don't let these assholes get away with this."

When *Gladiator*'s repairs began falling behind schedule, Al heeded Pearson's advice and called in the yard supervisor and the navy rep. He was quiet and reasonable—having learned from his father back in

Georgia that yelling and pounding the table are counterproductive— but he didn't mince words.

"Here's the deal," Al told them. He had notified port services that he would need tugboats on the day *Gladiator* was scheduled to leave the shipyard. Whether the repairs were finished or not, he would tow it out of the shipyard. They were not going to keep his ship. If they did not have the manpower and resources to complete the maintenance on schedule, another of the four shipyards in the area surely did. The government was paying to get the job done, and if the yard didn't do it on time, he would take away the contract.

"You can't do that," they told him. He was only the captain, and this was a United States Navy contract.

"It's my ship," Al shot back, "and I don't have to let you work on it. If I declare you persona non grata, then you can't work on my ship. And if you don't work on my ship, you don't get paid."

Gladiator was the first ship in the history of the MCM class to get out of a shipyard ahead of schedule. Al pulled this off because, unlike other MCM skippers, he refused to be intimidated and to play the shipyard people's games. They thought he was "only" a captain flailing against a navy contract. But Al knew he represented the navy's real interest—a fast, fairly priced turnaround. That certain knowledge gave him the clout to pull rank without fear of being overruled by his own superiors. In the end, Al won because both he and his adversaries knew he was right.

Yet again, Al Collins had demonstrated how a forthright and resourceful leader can conquer the system within a cyclopean organization.

LESSON: Let the system work for you.

After completing his command on *Gladiator,* Al wanted a quiet job back in San Diego while he waited for his next ship. Having been what the navy calls deep selected, or promoted to commander a year ahead of schedule, he could have written his own ticket. The assignment officer had a slot open in the personnel office in San Diego, but he said it wasn't a kingmaker position. "That's okay," said Al. "I'm not looking for a throne."

Partly because of me, Al's quiet life didn't last long. One day I invited him and my friend Jerry Huber, who was executive assistant to the admiral in San Diego, to join me for lunch. I proposed that Al take Jerry's job so that I could turn *Benfold* over to Jerry. Al said no way—he was laid back and happy and didn't need fourteen-hour days. A few weeks later, though, the admiral sat him down at Jerry's desk and said, "That's your new job." I doubt that Al was entirely surprised, but he knew the job was meant to be temporary.

Although Al had asked for a guided missile destroyer like *Benfold* at the next rotation of command, he didn't get it. When the orders came down, he had USS *Oldendorf,* a much older traditional destroyer. Al didn't complain. But when Admiral Edward Moore got the news, he took umbrage for him. What's the point of being deep selected, the admiral demanded, if you can't get your choice of ships? Moore's question was right on target. If younger officers saw that people who worked hard enough to be deep selected didn't get the promised reward, they would slack off.

The admiral called the seniormost officer in the assignment office and asked two more questions: Why didn't Al Collins get his first choice? And did anyone get a guided missile destroyer who had not been deep selected? When the officer called the admiral back, he didn't answer either question. He just wanted to know if Al would be satisfied with USS *Fitzgerald. Fitzgerald* was a guided missile destroyer, just as Al had requested—and he was satisfied.

Without making a fuss over what looked for all the world as if someone had given him the shaft, Al got the top brass to go to bat for him. Why? Because the admiral knew enough about Al and his achievements to know that someone had screwed up royally. What I particularly like about this story is that the admiral didn't go to bat for Al Collins because Al was some good ol' boy, a crony, or part of an insider network. No, the admiral acted because the assignment decision was dumb, perhaps discriminatory, and clearly against the navy's vital interest in developing sharp young captains.

Al was smart enough to know what would happen when the news reached the admiral—and patient enough to count on it.

LESSON: Greatness goes the extra mile.

When Al took command of *Fitzgerald,* it was already a very good ship. Scaling the heights to greatness was all that remained, but it would be a giant step.

Like *Benfold,* the ship was a fantastic fighting machine equipped with the Aegis missile-fire-control system. It was powered by four of the same type of jet engines used in DC-10 jetliners, so the huge ship could race along at more than thirty-one knots. Three more jet engines generated power for an astonishing array of sophisticated electrical equipment and futuristic weaponry. What is more, *Fitzgerald* made its own freshwater supply from seawater, and it was environmentally impeccable in putting nothing back into the sea that wasn't clean and biodegradable. To guard against chemical and biological attack, the ship's interior was kept at a slightly higher pressure than the outside atmosphere, which prevented toxic air from entering. *Fitzgerald* was nothing short of marvelous.

Unlike ships using other systems, Aegis-equipped vessels don't rely on separate radar systems for searching, tracking targets, and fire control. Instead, Aegis, a term derived from Greek mythology that today signifies "shield of the fleet," encases the ship in a radar bubble that is on constant alert to pick up anything hostile coming from any direction. Aegis can detect an intruder, identify it, assign the proper defensive weapon, and shoot it down—all automatically and within a few seconds.

Al had served on ships with older versions of guided-missile systems but he also knew a lot about Aegis. In fact, he was the man who had inspected *Fitzgerald*'s combat-system digital data-link program and certified it as combat ready. But he had never had any actual training or experience in running it. Nevertheless, he soon discovered that he knew a lot more about how the system worked than the men who operated it. That's not to say that they weren't smart and efficient. They were both, and they could run and maintain the system just fine. What they lacked was comprehensive knowledge about how it worked.

Al uncovered the same lack of deep-seated knowledge all over the ship. He had a sharp crew and good officers, but they couldn't explain how things worked, nor did they know why the navy way was the best way to do things.

Al being Al, he wasn't content with the status quo, even though it was a very good status quo. He wanted to improve *Fitzgerald* by making it great. He was dedicated to the cause of greatness, and he wanted his crew and professional officers to share his passion. He wanted them to come to know, without having to think about it, just how things should be done in the navy. In his first speech to the ship, he commended the crew for its very good achievements. He noted that for two years running, *Fitzgerald* had won the trophy for best ship in its battle group and squadron, a wonderful accomplishment. But now, Al said, let's go after the real prize: the Spokane Trophy for the most battle-ready ship in the entire Pacific Fleet.

Having gotten the crew's attention and sparked their enthusiasm, he started building a schedule aimed squarely at attaining the trophy. It involved constant practice with the weapons systems and flawless maintenance of the ship itself. Al also set out to snap up every minor award on the way to the trophy and to improve the ship's safety record. Within a few short months, *Fitzgerald* was honored by the chief of naval operations as the safest ship in the entire navy.

Al and his crew appeared to be steaming ahead toward the ultimate prize, but there were a few rocks in the stream, namely, the senior enlisted men. These were twenty or so chief petty officers who should have been among Al's most dependable allies, given that he himself had come up through the enlisted ranks. But the chiefs had managed to duck taking real responsibility for *Fitzgerald*'s problems, and they were now focused on protecting their own perks and privileges. They were skilled at it, but they thought small. Al was determined to broaden their horizons by enlisting them as yeomen in service to the cause of greatness on board *Fitzgerald*.

Having been a chief himself, Al could speak their language. "I would go down to their mess and say, 'Okay, guys, here we are; let's talk about this,'" he told me. And as he had done on *Gladiator*, he informed the chiefs that it was their job to train the junior officers. Even if some of the officers are pompous and won't listen, Al said, "Your job is still to train them and make sure that when we take this thing into battle, the officers are ready to go. You can't get around that." They heard him, but didn't necessarily heed him.

Indeed, Al didn't really get across his point about greatness until *Fitzgerald* was in Singapore on liberty. That coincided with a visit to Singapore by the chief of naval operations, who invited the officers and chiefs from all the ships in port to hear him explain his annual agenda of goals for the navy. Because *Fitzgerald* was on liberty, Al made attendance at the talk optional, and as he had expected, the delegation from his ship was sparse—perhaps five officers and two chiefs.

The next day Al called them to a meeting and explained their error. They had missed a chance to learn the goals and objectives of their organization, he said. They were supposed to be leaders, but they couldn't even tell their sailors what the navy expected of them. He could have made attendance at the talk mandatory, he noted, but that wasn't the point. He wanted them to take enough pride in themselves and their work to develop professionally of their own accord. He wanted the chiefs to want to learn on their own how to motivate shipmates to do what the navy wants them to do.

The lecture hit home. From then on, *Fitzgerald* was always well represented at similar events. More important, Al's people came to a true understanding of what he was talking about, largely because he underscored the message in subtle ways. He told his department heads that while the ship was in port, they could set their own hours just as long as they got their jobs done. However, anyone who wanted to work weekends or wanted the sailors to work weekends would have to get permission from him.

Professional pride is contagious, and pretty soon the whole crew was infected. That's why *Fitzgerald* won the Spokane trophy. Going beyond the mandatory in striving to be great is never easy, but it's always worth the effort. The lesson, you might say, is that pride goeth before the prize as well as after.

LESSON: Command with caution.

I've always been awed by soldiers who rush in where others hold back, but unless it's essential, I can't see much point to dying that way. I am far more impressed by leaders who pause to figure out exactly what victory will take, and only then go after it. If you have to bet your people's lives, make sure you have the best possible odds before you make your move.

That's what Al Collins did when *Fitzgerald* was in the Persian Gulf assigned to enforce the 1991 United Nations embargo on Iraqi oil sales. Smugglers in small ships would sneak out of Iraq with cargoes of oil and creep along the coast of Iran, trying to stay out of the international waters where *Fitzgerald* could legally stop them to inspect for contraband. The Iranians charged large tolls for the use of their territorial waters, but the potential profit made those tolls seem like a minor cost of doing business for the smugglers.

At a couple of points along the coast, shallow water forced the ships into international seas, where Al had boarders lying in wait in speedy inflatable boats called Zodiacs. At first the job looked as easy as collecting eggs from a henhouse. Stop and frisk; no sweat. But the smugglers had a lot at stake and were not exactly passive. They welded their hatches shut.

Expecting as much, the boarders had brought cutting torches, but they weren't powerful enough to burn through the thick metal. Al got stronger torches. The next group of boarders were able to cut through the doors, but when they did, the first man entering was sprayed with a Mace-like substance. The team was ready to fight—until their captain got wind of it. Al pulled his sailors off the ship and sent it on its way.

Al undoubtedly bought criticism in some quarters for taking a less than gung ho approach. But you won't hear any slams from me. I think he correctly judged the situation and decided that caution was indicated. These were new tactics for the smugglers. It made no sense to send his men and women into situations that presented unknown dangers. His admiral agreed, calling a halt to all boardings until the danger could be assessed. Al suggested using Navy SEAL units, an aquatic group specially trained for such situations, and that was how the job was handled thereafter. Using SEALs, *Fitzgerald* intercepted a record seventeen thousand metric tons of Iraqi oil. The use of appropriate force coupled with a bit of caution paid off.

LEADERS CAN BE DIVIDED INTO TWO GROUPS, OR SO IT seems to me. One type resembles a hare—fast off the mark, racing to who-knows-where but determined to get there first. Napoleon was just such a leader. He exuded brilliance, charisma, superiority, and world-beating aggressiveness—until his hubris led him to reach too far. First, he misjudged the strength of Russian resistance and was forced into a humiliating retreat, and then, with all of Europe aligned against him, he finally met his Waterloo. Few tears were shed at his demise.

The second type of leader is more of a tortoise—he knows exactly where he's going but takes a more cautious and deliberate route. Al Collins is just such a leader. He, too, exudes brilliance, charisma, and superiority—not superiority in an arrogant way, but superiority in his command of knowledge and technical expertise. He is a pragmatist and lifelong learner who wins by quickly zeroing in on the crux of an issue, setting a realistic course, and sticking to it until the problem is solved or the mission accomplished. Put another way, Al Collins doesn't "hope" he will achieve something he has set his mind to; hope is not his strategy. Instead, he puts the building blocks in place, trains his crew, and gives them the tools they need to deliver great results.

How did Al get to be a great leader? He took his mother's advice to become a great follower. So when the time came for him to lead, he knew exactly what to do. His method is well worth emulating.

LESSONS

Be realistic, not reckless.
Bide your time, and time your beefs.
When you need help, reach out.
Command with compassion.
Seize the day, and help others do the same.
Show off when you have to.
Make yourself a learning machine.
Figure out what's important, and act on it.
Make a contract with your people, and honor it.
Trust the crew to run the ship.
Make sure the whole crew is on board.
Use might to make right.
Let the system work for you.
Greatness goes the extra mile.
Command with caution.

CHAPTER 5

VP Laura Folse Is an Alchemist at BP

How does a small-town southern girl make good in the male-dominated world of oil and gas exploration? By combining brains, guts, and compassion with candor and a healthy dose of hard work.

A FULL THIRTY YEARS AFTER THE FEMINIST REBELLION, Americans of both sexes still do a double take when they see a woman in the leader's slot. The navy I grew up in had few women in ranks higher than mine. But if this attitude remains a handicap for many capable women, it was only a low hurdle for Laura Folse.

Growing up in little Moulton, Alabama, population three thousand, about ninety miles northwest of Birmingham, Laura had no preconceived notions about a "woman's role." Her folks, Spencer and Betty Waters, owned their own business, a local propane distributorship, and being a girl didn't exempt their daughter from hard, sometimes dirty, physical labor.

In a rural area like Moulton, people use propane to heat their chick-hatching houses, run farm equipment and household appliances, and even to heat and cool homes. So when Laura made service calls, she was right in the thick of hot and sweaty farm life. She even dug ditches and helped to install central air-conditioning systems, which few young women growing up in the 1960s and 1970s in Alabama—or any other state in the union—can lay claim to.

Laura felt no intellectual limits either, and she had no qualms about pursuing her love of science. A self-proclaimed science nerd, she was one of only a few women, maybe two out of twenty students, studying geology at Auburn University. But then, in the Waters family both the boys and the girls were encouraged to pursue higher education. Laura told me that for nearly twenty consecutive years, her parents had at least one of their four children, sometimes two, in college at the same time. The family's shared love of learning has produced a slew of advanced degrees. Laura and her three siblings all have at least one masters, while two boast a pair of them and one also holds a Ph.D. Laura herself has masters degrees in both geology and business management.

Her early exposure to the rough-and-tumble world of physical labor and male-dominated scientific achievement has helped to make Laura a gutsy yet compassionate leader at the oil giant Amoco (now part of London-based BP PLC). The company hired her twenty years ago, right out of graduate school, to trek around the world looking for energy sources. Invoking visions of Indiana Jones—but without his requisite evil antagonists and perilous chase scenes—Laura actually took her rock hammer and sample bag to Asia in search of prospective oil and gas deposits. After working her way up to ever greater responsibilities and picking up managerial experience along the way, Laura is now BP's vice president of technology and one of its senior leaders.

Asked to describe herself, Laura said she is very self-directed, someone who draws her energy "largely from within," but who truly enjoys teamwork. "To me, there is nothing better than working with a group of people toward a common goal," she told me. And her team knows, she said, that "I would fight any fight and take any bullet for them." No wonder Laura has earned praise as an exceptional leader.

But hard work and uncommon success in a male-dominated world are not the only things that mark Laura Folse as someone who excites people to adopt her vision and follow her toward a common goal. To become the leader she is today, Laura has trudged through periods of self-doubt and a good deal of critical assessment about what motivates her and what traits keep her from performing at her peak. After one such crisis, an epiphany came when Laura realized that her self-imposed fear of what others might think of her was her worst enemy. She was who she was, she decided, and there was no point in trying to hide it or pretend to be someone else. After she had wholeheartedly embraced what she calls her truth, Laura's fear evaporated and she was soon back on track to being the confident, team-oriented, fun-loving, consultative leader who has done so well throughout her career.

Laura's achievement has been tempered with heartache and personal loss, but amazingly, she has used that loss to shore up her determination to never again live in fear. Not long ago, her husband, Dan, died of lung cancer. Dan was a healthy, active man who worked as a carpenter and never smoked. The shock of his Stage 4 cancer diagnosis and his subsequent rapid decline could easily have left Laura angry and bewildered, even fearful again. Instead, she told me that having survived this ordeal, "I am not afraid of anything anymore. How can I even begin to believe that I am living a full life and doing what I was put here to do if I live in fear?" She hopes to communicate to her teenage son the importance of taking control of your life and never surrendering it to trivial concerns or baseless fears.

As for being a leader in all its ramifications, Laura summed up her deepest personal feelings for me this way: "It's an ongoing, fascinating journey. The journey is inspiring, yet it is also difficult some days—how complex it can feel, how tiring it can be to listen deeply, to serve upward, downward, and sideways, to keep finding the courage to push against the traditional corporate tide, to experience people who pull on us because they feel like victims, to be a single mom in all of this, and to stay authentic and centered throughout it all. Some days, fear does win, and I choose the baseline behaviors and become more controlling. This makes me know, down deep inside, the importance of creating space for personal well-being, nourishment, and regeneration—and the consequences when I don't, when the universe whacks me with its two-by-four and hands me days where it takes a great deal of courage just to show up. I cherish this path I'm on because every instance allows me to know myself a bit better. And the better I know myself, the better I can help others to know themselves. And to me that is what true, authentic leadership is about."

I hope you are as impressed and intrigued with Laura Folse as I am. I think that after hearing her expand on the vision of leadership she so eloquently outlined above and studying her leadership lessons in the pages just ahead, you will come away determined to fashion yourself in her image as a more self-aware and team-oriented leader, honest with both yourself and your team. Let's get to those lessons.

LESSON: To attract followers, share the lead.

In the early years of Laura's career at Amoco, she was part of a group that ferreted out promising geological data in areas of the world not then being explored for oil and gas. One assignment took her to Laos to do purely scientific fieldwork; she and her team combed riverbeds for rock outcroppings that could be broken apart and analyzed for traces of oil and gas.

Laura was the project leader of this team of field geologists and experts in various subspecialties, each of whom reported to a different boss. Each morning, though, before the group headed out to the day's work site, it was Laura who, after consulting with the others, gave advance instructions about the following day's program to the Laotian guide, the security people, and the local geologist. But at the end of every single day, she told me, "After I had gone back to my hotel room, the head Laotian person would call one of the men just to verify that what I had told them was correct."

Was a sexist attitude to blame? It was partly that and partly her relative youth, Laura said. (The others weren't a lot older, she added, but they looked it because "they were the classic, shaggy-looking geologists wearing hairy-toed sandals.") The problem was really a cultural one, Laura said, in that "the Laotians didn't realize my instructions were based on prior consultation with my team." They just couldn't imagine that a woman, and a young one at that, would be involved in consultation with men.

I've known some people who, in Laura's position, would have been angry at such lack of respect. But I think it's a total waste of energy to get upset and angry about things you can't control, especially a cultural issue like the one Laura encountered. It makes a lot more sense to tie your sense of self-satisfaction to something you can control, like producing great results. Just submerge your ego and figure out a way to do the job you're being paid for, which is what she did with such apparent ease.

Hardly anyone doubts Laura Folse these days. In her position as a technology vice president at BP, she leads seven hundred professionals who are research-and-development scientists and engineers and in-house technical consultants. BP relies on Laura to make sure its exploration and production technology equals or exceeds industry standards. Her responsibilities have mushroomed over the years, but one thing, at least, has not changed: she still consults with her team before making most decisions.

The secret of Laura's success, then and now, is her conviction that "I'm not smart enough to do it by myself." The best way for a leader to get a team working together, to inspire them to buy into a common goal and realize their full potential, is to create an open, trusting environment of equals in which everyone, team members as well as leaders, feels accountable for the work.

"I don't see the leadership role as standing on a mountaintop and issuing great words," Laura told me. "I think the main role of a leader is to see that people are communicating with each other and to make sure they have what they need. My job is to glue the pieces together, to hold the whole."

In Laos, she said, "we had such an open relationship within the team. The guys told me what was happening; they knew I wasn't going to try to tell them how to do their jobs. They trusted me and backed me up, and I backed them up with the bosses. There was never an issue about my being a woman."

In her current post, Laura supervises all sorts of scientific wizards, including Ph.D. physicists, who talk to her about solving mathematical problems by going through wormholes to another dimension. "I don't add value by checking on their work—I couldn't check their work. That would be absolutely ludicrous," she readily admitted. "I add value by being clear on the team's direction, helping them understand the boundaries they are working in, and doing my best to ensure they have the space and support they need."

Her background as a geologist is a major asset when it comes to managing diverse teams, Laura believes. "What I know how to do is think systemically. I can see patterns in complex systems and weave the threads together," she said. It's something geologists are very good at, probably because they have to know a little bit about every science, from physics to chemistry to math to biology and zoology. "Geology is one of those sciences that puts it all together," Laura continued, and being able to do that "helps me to help [my teammates] determine what their priorities should be."

Laura has become a wizard in her own right at understanding the big picture and helping individuals and teams to see where they fit into the BP strategy as a whole. "Some of the best leaders I have seen," she told me, "are those who actually know little detail about what they are leading but understand the big picture really well." She has also learned how to block out the noise and the politics present in every large organization so that her people can do their work unimpeded.

All this gives her teams powerfully positive feelings toward Laura and the company. In everything they do, including making all sorts of technical breakthroughs, her people show that they see themselves not as wage slaves but as committed and responsible team members, ready and eager to go the extra mile.

There was a moment in Laura's career when, as she put it, "I kind of lost my legs." Amoco had just merged with BP and she was adjusting to the new environment. One of her new colleagues from BP took her on a walk and gave her some well-intended advice: she needed to behave more like BP's traditional command-and-control leaders. Fearful of being seen as a weak leader, Laura began ordering people around, telling them what they should and shouldn't do—in other words, micromanaging. "I was not developing the leaders under me at all because I wasn't willing to follow anybody," she said. "I must have been an awful person to work for. I was leading from a place of fear and using fear to motivate others."

Terribly unhappy with her situation, Laura, without the knowledge of BP, sought out the help of an external coach. After much introspection and reflection, Laura began to realize why she was not building a high-performing team and why her team leaders came to her with the most trivial of matters. The answer: by wielding an authoritarian stick, she had set up the expectation within the team that decisions were not something to be made in consultation, but were her sole province. She also realized that this was not her natural style; she had allowed someone else to use fear to make her completely alter her leadership approach.

What Laura learned can be simply stated: real leaders don't so much lead as follow, staying tuned to the needs and problems of their team, listening to find out how to inspire the team to greater effort and innovation. In Laura's words, "Real leaders aren't afraid to follow because that is how they develop the leaders of the future."

LESSON: Bust a gut to redeem misfits.

Laura almost never jumps to conclusions and seldom misses an opportunity to help a floundering team member get back on track. She is so good at turning underperformers into team superstars that she could be called an alchemist. The major difference is that while these medieval philosophers and scientists only dreamed of turning base metals into gold, Laura has actually found the formula.

She starts with the conviction that "every person is sacred, and no one's path in life is any more important than anyone else's." She sees her leadership mission as one of matching people with the work that can make them happy. So when one of her team members is not doing well in his job, she does not assume that the person is lazy, stubborn, or simply not up to the task. Instead, Laura looks for the disconnect between what the person wants and what he is getting out of his work.

Just as I found on *Benfold,* that takes a lot of careful listening. "I sit down with them," Laura explained, "and I try to find a way to help them get the satisfaction they need in their work, or to bring something to their work that will give them satisfaction." Sometimes, there is no obvious solution, and she finds the person a different assignment or lets her or him go. "The worst thing you can do in a firm is to leave a bad manager in place," she said.

Invoking a vivid image, Laura told me she tries to approach such sessions by imagining she has "to fire Mother Teresa"—a method that at least establishes a loving atmosphere. "If you do it from a place of love and care," she added, "I can't remember an instance where the person didn't actually thank me for putting them out of their misery."

More often than not, though, these discussions lead to changes that give the unhappy worker a new opportunity to perform as a responsible team member, thus rejuvenating her performance.

Laura told me about a conversation with a man on her team—call him John—a longtime BP employee whose work and attitude were poor. Laura described John as "a bit of an energy vampire," someone who saw himself as a victim of everyone else's mistakes. He sucked the energy right out of Laura with his chronic laundry list of complaints.

After calling John in for a discussion, Laura began by telling him: "I want you to know that I care for you as a person. Some of the things I have to say are likely to hurt you, but it is not about whether or not you are a kind, loving, important person, which you are." Then she identified the issue as his poor job performance and spoke about specific problems.

What she said was not really new to John. "You never get to this point," Laura explained, without first having had "lead-up conversations around what you need from the person and what he needs from you." Realizing that he had been failing her as well as himself, John wept. When the interview was over, he asked if he could hug Laura.

These conversations are never easy, and in this particular case,

Laura also had to tell John that his job was being redefined and that he would no longer be reporting to her. But she provided encouragement by offering to pay for outside coaching to help him work through some of his personal issues. John accepted the offer and, gradually, his entire attitude has changed. He has done "absolutely mind-boggling" work since then, Laura said.

Now when she runs into John, Laura told me, he will stop her and say, "I wish someone had had the guts twenty years ago to tell me what you did."

Glossing over someone's failures is highly damaging in the long run, Laura believes. If you accept the notion of individual sacredness, then you owe it to your people, as a concerned leader, to "tell them what you are really saying at the water cooler." In fact, letting people know they are not meeting your expectations is a real act of kindness, as long as it's done with the right motivation.

Not everyone is comfortable with the notion of love and caring in the workplace, of course. It works for Laura because it's consistent with her character. My sailors certainly knew that I cared about them, but all of us would have begun to squirm if I'd told them I loved them. You have to express your concern and appreciation for your followers in ways that feel right to you and them.

I agree 100 percent that poor performers can't be allowed to keep muddling along without some intervention from their leaders. For one thing, tolerating mediocrity (or worse) sends a terrible signal to the vast majority of your crew members who are busting a gut for you. It's easy to get demoralized when you see some folks slacking off while you're working your butt off. Pretty soon the entire crew will start emulating the slackers. And why not if there don't seem to be any consequences?

I remember a situation on *Albert David,* my first ship, where nearly the whole group of junior officers got the wrong signal because the captain was not only an abusive leader but a poor teacher. It wasn't that we were slackers, just that he treated us as if we were—and then did nothing to help us mend whatever fault he found with us.

On one particular night, he decided to declare open season on the bridge watch standers, berating his junior officers on a whim. The first of three watch teams was having problems, largely because it was so difficult maneuvering within the tight confines of the battle group's formation. But the captain, as usual, just blew his top and made no effort to help the team work through a tough situation. He loudly declared that they were all nitwits and ordered up the reliefs. Calling up the reliefs means the previous team has just been fired, at least temporarily, and it's extremely humiliating.

So the second team of watch standers took over, but in less than thirty minutes the captain was yelling at them too. He called for the next, and last, group of reliefs, which included me. But this time, rather than feeling humiliated, everyone was thinking, "Hey, dude, the problem isn't with us, it's with you or with the situation. Maybe you, as the captain, should step up to help."

When the captain called up my group, we figured we'd be fired in a matter of minutes, after which he'd have no choice but to go back to the original team. In the end, we didn't actually get fired, because the captain finally calmed down. Realizing that he'd screwed up the whole watch rotation, he told the first crew to "take your watch back."

The whole situation bordered on comical, except that the captain lost all credibility as a result. Gratifying though that was to those who suffered under his poor leadership, it wasn't good for the ship.

In stark contrast, when Laura Folse decides to confront someone with an honest assessment of his poor performance, she also works with him to find the cause of the problem and a solution. If, for whatever reason, the person can't accept the assessment or won't work on changing, he must be fired—but always in a caring manner. People who've been let go usually show relief and even gratitude, Laura said, because they've been suffering too.

When a person accepts your agreed-on solution and improves his performance and on-the-job behavior, then you are responsible for making sure that from then on he is judged on what he is doing now, not on what he used to do. Bad reputations are hard to shake. A leader like Laura is careful to give praise where it is due, and correct anyone who judges a shipmate by past performance.

Over her years of leadership, Laura has earned her reputation as an alchemist. Paradoxically, her reward has been to be stuck with a lot of seeming losers: people with performance issues somehow always end up at her desk. "One of the greatest compliments I was ever given," she recalled, "was a performance review that said something like, 'Laura is able to develop anyone.'" If so, she told me, it's only because she respects people and their various motivations and concerns, and does not have a hierarchy of caring. When people understand that, they are truly able to listen and learn from her without the usual defensiveness that we all feel when we're called on the carpet.

Every time Laura transforms another weak team member into an enthusiastic one, one who takes responsibility for the work and constantly pushes the envelope, the alchemist is truly minting gold for the employee and for her company.

Like Laura, I personally sat down with people who were having performance problems and tried to help them work out a solution. Telling someone their work stinks is one of the toughest things a captain has to do, but these conversations are critical for the person involved and for the overall morale of the ship. Mediocrity or downright failure can be a virus that spreads all through the organization.

The thing you have to remember is that everyone on board knows who the slackers are, and they're just watching and waiting to see how you're going to handle it. The tricky part is in making it clear that you will not tolerate mediocrity, while also reassuring your crew that you still care about the slacker and will do nothing to humiliate him— that, in fact, you will do everything in your power to help him get back on track.

There is actually a process in place in the navy that seems to mystify many of the corporate types I know: it works to identify poor performers and then gives them a fair chance to change their ways. After a deficiency is identified, the sailor gets a chance to talk about it with the chain of command, which offers whatever help is needed to correct the problem. But if the sailor can't make the needed changes within a specified time, say four or six months, she or he is told to be ready to pack the duffel bags and go elsewhere.

On *Benfold* we tried counseling sessions first, and if that didn't work, the problem traveled up the chain of command until it landed in my lap. I remember one sailor, a radioman, who reported for duty halfway through my tour and quickly racked up too many visits with me. We did everything we could to connect with this guy, but nothing worked. Three of my best people, Radioman First Class John Rafalko, Second-Class Petty Officer David Pike, and Chief Petty Officer Janice Harris all went out of their way to help the kid.

You may remember Rafalko from *It's Your Ship*. As I described in that book, clogged communication channels were commonplace when I joined the navy. Sometimes the problems were serious enough to threaten an entire mission. An equipment failure nearly scuppered the whole Gulf fleet during the Iraqi crisis of 1997. Thanks to *Benfold's* own John Rafalko and his brilliant solution, we were rescued from a wartime crisis.

The radioman's most critical function at sea is to establish a communication channel by patching in all the frequencies to the radios and then connecting the radios to the antennas so you can transmit and receive voice communications. He also keys in the code that encrypts the transmissions, which makes the radio shack a top-secret space.

Typically, radio shacks are not hotbeds of performance because the operators have a difficult time maintaining the equipment at sea—particularly the antennas, which tend to corrode. When that happens, the quality of the communication deteriorates. But what you don't always know is who's at fault—you or the ship you're trying to communicate with. The tendency, or course, is to blame the other guy—rightly or wrongly. On *Benfold,* though, we had such a top-notch group of radiomen, headed by Rafalko and Pike and supervised by the extremely effective Janice Harris, that we were almost always right when we said the problem was not with us.

Anyway, the young man whom even Rafalko, Pike, and Harris couldn't turn around was assigned to us by the Bureau of Naval Personnel. But from day one, he didn't fit in. His personal hygiene was lousy. He wasn't willing to pull his weight. He seemed determined to be a failure—and he succeeded in a big way.

One day the misfit was discovered in the radio shack with his own personal computer hooked up to his AOL account. Now taking your PC into the radio space is absolutely forbidden in order to prevent the unauthorized transmission of the top-secret encryption codes. Most of the major spying events of the last two or three decades have involved radio personnel and encryption codes.

I had to report this lapse of security to the commodore. Transmitting code over an AOL account is an automatic violation of security regulations, and it's so serious that a captain who reports even a suspected violation may be knocked out of the running for the Battle E award and also for the Spokane Trophy. Obviously, consequences like that encourage some people in the chain of command to keep quiet about possible security lapses.

If a similar thought even fleetingly crossed my mind, I knew I couldn't keep quiet about what had happened. For one thing, the guy might actually have been transmitting secret code. For another, all the radiomen knew about it. I couldn't risk sending a signal that such breaches could ever be overlooked.

I was furious, but without delay I reported what had happened to the commodore. I also told him what we were doing to determine whether any secret information had been transmitted. He thanked me for owning up to the problem, and asked me to keep him informed on the outcome of the investigation.

Fortunately, the culprit gave us total access to his computer, so we were able to check everything he had received and sent out since coming aboard. A thorough scan of his computer ruled out espionage.

I immediately reduced his rank, but he was still entitled to receive counseling and be informed of his deficiencies. I gave him six months to shape up or literally ship out. My command was changed before the six months were up, but the kid did not improve and was finally separated from the navy. Unfortunately, not every misfit can be redeemed.

LESSON: Cover your assets.

Laura Folse routinely "steps in the middle" when a member of her team runs afoul of a top manager, or "when senior people launch grenades by e-mail, a pretty cowardly way to launch a grenade, by the way." Her team knows that she would defend them in any battle, Laura had told me. But it's doubtful that they ever imagined how far she would actually go.

Probably her greatest exploit came in a pitched battle some years back over the design of her team's offices. Other than pay, there is no single more emotional issue for most workers. "John Browne [BP's CEO] pays me to be a big leader in this firm," Laura explained, "and I believe that office space should serve the employees and not vice versa."

Management had laid down a set of universal guidelines as to how the space in the building was to be set up, and Laura's people were up in arms over it. She, in turn, was concerned about the negative impact the new environment might have on her staff's performance. She also worried that her team might slip into what she calls "victim mode," thinking that neither the team's nor Laura's spheres of influence could trump corporate standards and bureaucracy when it came to something like office space.

Determined to demonstrate that her spheres of influence are infinite, Laura, all on her own, hired an environmental geographer to find out how her team members related to their work space and what each wanted the space to look like. Then, consensus in hand, she hired another consultant to redo the conference room, meanwhile asking a friend in charge of office space to just look the other way for a few days.

The consultant created a Mediterranean café setting with water features and round picnic tables with chairs. She painted the walls a different color and changed the carpet. Some of Laura's people loved the space, others hated it, she told me, but all agreed on its impact. They thought the shock value of the remodeling demonstrated the power of testing boundaries and taking a firm stand on matters of importance to the team.

After visiting Laura in her offices in Aberdeen, Scotland, I could understand the team's reaction. We men—and for what it's worth, Laura was heading up a male-dominated team at the time—are often accused of being oblivious to any place that doesn't feature cold beer and a TV set tuned to a sports channel. But this place was hard to ignore.

What a kick! No drab executive boxes here. Her conference room, in particular, was way out of the ordinary. It was furnished with beach chairs and a table covered by an umbrella. The room itself was so much fun to be in that I could imagine meetings in this space being fun too. Some people are more affected by their surroundings than others, but I think a conference room like Laura's could definitely spark some out-of-the-box thinking. The juxtaposition of work and play tools in the same room reflected Laura's own philosophy. "I take my job seriously and I am deeply motivated by the pursuit of excellence in business," she told me. "I just think that delivering shareholder value and having fun are complementary rather than mutually exclusive. In case you're wondering, the 'wacky' conference room cost only slightly more than the old drab one, and I have no doubt we earned the difference back the first week."

Not surprisingly, Laura's bold action sent ripples through the entire building. Even people in other departments who hated the changes were impressed by Laura's willingness to go to bat for her team. "I knew beforehand that the team liked and trusted me," she said, "but they thought there wasn't much I could do about the office space problem. Essentially, I was saying, 'There's no limit to what I'll do, the risks I'll take, if it's important to my team.'"

Laura's willingness to buck management's heavy-handed pronouncements demonstrated the courage of a true leader. Only someone with a deep-seated commitment to her team would so blatantly ignore management's decree. At the same time, Laura made it clear that this was not simply a power play, and that leaders don't break rules unless a larger purpose is served. In effect, she was saying, "My responsibilities as a leader spur me to find new and better solutions, and that's the way it should be. But actions like mine require a really good reason to work around company regulations. I'm a manager, not a cowgirl."

When I commanded *Benfold,* some people thought we broke all sorts of rules. We didn't. We had guidelines, and we lived within the spirit of those guidelines. What we did was to modify them to fit our own needs and our own situation.

You have to remember why you're in a leadership role in the first place. The CEO hired or promoted you because of your sound judgment. Regardless of how many rules and regulations an organization churns out, no rule book can cover every situation, nor should it. That would make life so boring. Being a manager would be downright awful if all you did was follow a rule book. Heck, you wouldn't even need midlevel managers or navy captains.

Fortunately, that's not the way things work. There are always gray areas that need interpreting. Laura used her good judgment to decide that an offbeat interior-decorating scheme might be just the thing to lift up her team. And it was.

Laura imagined that her team would be pleased with her gutsy move, but what she couldn't have foreseen was the impact it would have on the metrics used to gauge employee satisfaction. From a rather low reading when Laura arrived in the organization, her team's satisfaction ranking surged to the top of the charts in less than two years. And, at the same time, performance also improved—all because Laura sent a signal that she not only listened to what her team had to say, but she was also ready to do all she could to keep them satisfied.

LESSON: Crap work is a matter of attitude.

Laura is always on the alert for discontent among her team members. Into each life a little crap work must fall, and most people will tell you that much too much has fallen into theirs. But Laura takes issue with the very concept. As vice president of technology, she has her share of tasks she likes less than others, but she takes these chores in stride— they're all part of the job.

She believes that coping with crap work is all a matter of attitude. To help her people cope, a leader can let them know she is aware their jobs involve some crap work, and guide them to see how that work is nevertheless contributing to the overall delivery of business results for the whole team. Above all, Laura stressed, a leader should thank them for their contributions.

She herself regularly sends handwritten notes to her colleagues—up the command chain, at her same level, and below her. Laura explained that the notes are simply a way of connecting to another person— perhaps by providing a word of encouragement or acknowledging something the recipient has done or offering a bit of Laura's self-deprecating humor. "I think that note writing, particularly thank-you notes, is a dying art," she said, adding: "It's a shame because I am amazed at the impact it has. People regularly tell me how much it meant to them that someone in my position took the time to write a note congratulating them on a good piece of work. I find it very humbling. I simply want to thank them for what they bring to the team and let them know that I know it's not always easy, and that all our work involves parts that are, well, crappy.

"I believe that the quality of your life is determined by the quality of your thinking," Laura went on. So the underlying issue for a leader is to change a team's negative feelings about a job to positive ones. Sometimes all it takes is a thank you. Positive feelings translate to a sense of responsibility for the enterprise and its work. And when your people truly assume responsibility, they shift into overdrive, working harder and better, breaking new ground. The result: big performance gains.

When it comes to crap work on a navy ship, the boatswain's mates who do the deck work, the chipping and painting, may lay claim to having the crappiest job on the ship. But I could make a case for a job that meets the criteria both literally and figuratively.

First, a little background. *Benfold*'s sewage system consisted of eight pumps divided into two separate areas with four pumps each. Poorly designed mechanical seals on these pumps were constantly breaking down, raising the likelihood of a sewage emergency in which we would not have been able to process sewage or pump it over the side. A scary scenario—and one that kept me thinking about sewage more often, I would wager, than virtually any other captain in the U.S. Navy. I was obsessed with making sure we had enough additional mechanical seals to allow us to fix any problem ourselves—a job that would truly qualify as crappy.

Besides my focus on spare parts, I also spent a lot of time in the contaminated holding-tank pump room, talking to the single technician trained to maintain these pumps. Every other day I'd descend into the bowels of the ship, climbing hand over hand down the railings in a grimy space about half the size of an elevator shaft. Sailors have fallen and broken their backs making this climb. It's difficult, dirty, dangerous, and in heavy seas, well, you can just imagine.

The sailor I went to see down there was one Shaun Perkins. Here was a guy working in really crappy conditions, and I couldn't do much for him other than to let him know that I knew what a great job he was doing and that I really depended on him. I think he appreciated it. And as a result of my interest and my telling him that we couldn't operate the ship without him, he seemed to take great pride in doing his crap work. I couldn't make his working conditions any better, but I could make him feel better about his job—maybe make it slightly less crappy.

Hardly anyone would have guessed it, but when Shaun Perkins took the SAT test we offered on *Benfold,* he scored 1,290—a lot of people would kill for a score like that. Here was a sailor who spent his days at the bottom of a shaft maintaining a ship's sewage system, and he scored higher on the SATs than thousands of seniors attending very prestigious high schools.

After Shaun had started taking college courses on *Benfold,* I was walking through the mess decks around midnight one night and found him reading a textbook. Knowing what a smart kid he was, I was curious about what he was studying. I was shocked to hear, "Philosophy." When I asked what other courses he was taking, he said, "Psychology." Now I was really dumbfounded. With his brains and technical skills, I figured he was wasting his time. Because of my own prejudices, I was predisposed to see him doing something else, something that would pay more and make use of his enviable talents.

As it turned out, Shaun earned a civil engineering degree from a Southern California university. His foray into psychology and philosophy helped him decide that neither was his true calling. Today he works as a civil engineer.

LESSON: Let your team paint its own vision.

Laura Folse has little patience with leaders who proclaim from on high the vision and corporate goals that all employees should share. To Laura, vision is linked to motivation. But "I don't have a clue about what motivates other people," she said. "I do know what motivates me." So when Laura talks to her team about its goals, she describes the process of getting there in terms of painting a picture. Each team member, based on his or her personal motivation, adds brushstrokes until the vision comes into being.

"The brushstrokes that I put on the painting are the things that get me out of bed every day and give me my spiritual nourishment," Laura told me. "I invite [my teammates] to tell me what their brushstrokes are." In that way, she and her team members learn what is most important to one another, what motivates them.

"The real way to build a quality business," said Laura, "is to find out what nourishes people, what they look for at their jobs. Some look for achievement. Some look for a place to attach an umbilical cord and have a sense of community. Some want nothing more than the cash, and you need to respect that. Of course, you don't try to build a community around people who don't want to be part of it."

When you understand the motivations that govern your team members' work attitudes and performance, you can help them meet those goals by adjusting their working conditions, their assignments, even their hours. It is the surest way to inspire your team to look at its work with an owner's perspective. Once your people take responsibility for reaching your common goals, once they see themselves as owners rather than underlings, they will stretch the definition of the possible. Naturally, the painting that Laura and her team will produce has some constraints: "There are the boundaries around ethics, some sense of fairness, and the fact that we all work for a firm—a group of shareholders. We have to be profitable."

Within those limits, though, the vision will grow, reflecting the inspirations and enthusiasms of the individual team members. As such, it will be vastly more meaningful than anything issued from a mountaintop.

LESSON: Help keep your band on key.

In a sports-obsessed society like America's, words like *first, best,* and *winner* pepper conversations in every realm, especially business. Is winning important? Sure. But paradoxically, if you fail to understand the true meaning of being first and the responsibilities that go along with the number-one position, you may hobble your team's ability to win. Laura learned that when she was just a girl.

A standout performer in her Alabama high school marching band, Laura worked long and hard to capture the first-chair position in the flute section. It was a top-ranked band that had appeared at events all across the country, so the distinction earned Laura, as she puts it, "some slight individual recognition." But she soon figured out just how unimportant her position was when it really counted: during an actual performance. The band "depended on every single person performing at his or her best," Laura said. "It doesn't matter if your first chair is outstanding if your fifteenth chair isn't also delivering on that day."

In business too, your team is never going to realize its full potential until all the members take pride in their work and become fully responsible for their actions, giving their best performance every day and always looking for new ways to improve it. If one or two members play off key, whether they are the stars or lesser lights, the team itself and the organization as a whole will suffer.

So how can you make sure that every member of your band is playing in the right key? Again, Laura learned the answer in that high school band. It turned out that being first chair was more about taking responsibility than basking in the glory of being number one. Although never really spelled out, she told me, the implicit message "in everything we did was that part of my job as first chair was to help the rest of the flute section."

Laura had to be careful, of course. "I didn't go around saying I was really good and asking if they wanted help," she recalled. "But rather, since I was going to spend some time working on a particularly difficult section of a piece, I would ask if they would be interested in working with me." By taking that humble approach, Laura helped boost not only the flute section's performance, but also the performance of the band as a whole. "Humility is very important when you're in a leadership role," she declared.

By treating her position as an opportunity to improve her team's playing, she took on overall responsibility herself, behaving with the focused interest and initiative of a leader. She also served as an example to her team of how the right attitude can increase anyone's enjoyment and sense of achievement.

I should note that when Laura went on to play in the band at Auburn University, she had a very different experience. In a band filled with gifted people who were studying for a career in music, she was far from being first chair. In fact, she was pretty far down in the pecking order of flutists. But the crucial lessons she'd learned in her high school band still held true: Every single player, playing his or her best, was essential to the success of the band as a whole. Keeping that thought in mind, Laura said she "never felt second class" in the college band, "even though I clearly was, relative to everyone else."

How can you convince everyone on your team, the least important as well as the most, to take responsibility for the team's performance?

Help them to understand that pecking orders are counterproductive, that everyone on the team is vital to anyone's success. Indeed, to recast an old saying, every band is only as good as its lesser players.

LESSON: Remember who you are.

At a young age, Laura had already carved an impressive career for herself at Amoco when it became a part of giant BP. As a leader and a musician, she had long been a true believer in teams and teamwork and the consultative model. On the well-meaning advice of a colleague, however, she felt she had to instantly transform herself into "an all-knowing, all-seeing, very directive leader." That, she had been led to believe, was what BP expected her to be. She tried, but she was a bust. More important, Laura was miserably unhappy trying to shoehorn herself into a leadership style that didn't suit her personality.

Feeling like a misfit, Laura began to send signals to the outside world that she was interested in leaving BP. In short order, the recruiters began calling. Realizing, Laura said, that she had "lost the plot," the approach to leadership that had carried her so far so fast, she decided to go into these interviews with her mask off. "I was going to let them see who I was," she told me. "Yes, I would tell them that I wanted to be part of a high-performing company, but what I really cared about was how you get the performance. The way I got good performance for myself was by playing to the meaningfulness of the work, its importance to the world, and how much fun it was." That was the real Laura, the leader who, in the past, had inspired her teams to take responsibility for their jobs, to far outstrip their previous performances, and to enjoy the experience.

At first, Laura feared that her attitude might put off the recruiting interviewers. But she found that they liked it, and several wanted to carry on the recruiting process. As her confidence began to return, the truth of the situation dawned: "I started realizing that the barrier to my doing the stuff I wanted to do at work had nothing to do with BP's culture. It had everything to do with me, about how I relate to and worry about what other people think. I was afraid of being judged harshly or losing my job. I finally realized that if that was the worst thing that could happen to me, then it wasn't such a big deal. The fear evaporated." Laura turned down one offer, called off the rest of the interviews, and decided to stay at BP. "I also committed myself to further developing my self-awareness so that I could bring my authentic leadership style to work every day," she told me.

Not long after, with her confidence and focus renewed, Laura filled out a BP questionnaire about her career goals, a self-analysis required of the company's top executives. Instead of the typical response along the lines of "I want to learn the job I'm doing and then take the next senior job and then become CEO," Laura wrote that she was not motivated by "positional power," but by being able to receive "my spiritual nourishment through my work, and to have lots of fun in the process." She viewed any future positions she might receive as the natural outcome, and not goals unto themselves.

After sending the form along, Laura received an emergency phone call from another well-meaning friend who was also one of the company's top officers. He urged her to change her response before it went to the top executives. He said it had not been written in "the normal BP way," and he was worried for her. She refused, saying, "If they don't want me as a member of leadership because of what I wrote, it would be a good thing for me to know that."

But those executives apparently had a different reaction. Instead of showing her the door, they chose to send her to Stanford University to study for a master's degree in management. It was quite a feather in her cap. Stanford is one of John Browne's alma maters, and he interviews and endorses every candidate that BP sends. Only one or two people make the cut each year. Once Laura completed her degree, the company gave her a promotion that led to her current vice presidency.

When Laura got her groove back, she became happy in her work again and also started getting phenomenal results from her team. When I first met Laura, it was May, but her unit's productivity goals for the entire year had already been met. Everyone was still doing the same amount of work, but they were working smarter and more efficiently, which led them to meet twelve months of profit and production goals in less than half that time.

In the military, there are definite behavior and leadership expectations—many of them unwritten and often self-imposed. It's easy to get all wrapped up in being the leader you think the organization wants while submerging the real you, the person you were meant to be. I didn't really start to blossom until I figured out what kind of a leader Mike Abrashoff wanted to become, instead of trying to squeeze myself into some one-size-fits-all navy-captain mold. That's when the successes started to pile up. People can sense genuineness and authenticity, and that's what they truly respond to.

LAURA FOLSE'S SUPERB LEADERSHIP SKILLS ARE MOST EVIdent in her skill at leading teams, her talent for helping people in trouble, her self-confidence, and her stand-up courage. But all of them are rooted in her forthright way of dealing with people, beginning with herself. To its credit, BP recognized that. Her personal authenticity is central to convincing her teammates to follow her lead and take an all-out attitude toward their jobs, and that is the true gold she mines for BP.

Having consistently put her faith in consultative, team-oriented leadership since her early days of globe-trotting with a diverse team of geologists, Laura is never afraid to admit that she doesn't know it all. Her humility and truthfulness, combined with her obvious concern for people and her willingness to go to bat for her team, have made Laura Folse a standout at BP. She proves, as do so many others profiled in this book, that being true to yourself works like magic in drawing people to your cause and making them want to help you achieve it.

LESSONS

To attract followers, share the lead.
Bust a gut to redeem misfits.

Cover your assets.
Crap work is a matter of attitude.
Let your team paint its own vision.
Help keep your band on key.
Remember who you are.

CHAPTER 6

Officer-in-Charge Ward Clapham Transforms the Mounties

Speak softly and carry a hockey stick is an apt motto for a cop whose insightful approach to leadership has paid big dividends in communities around the world.

WARD CLAPHAM IS A MOUNTIE. IF THAT CONJURES UP A square-jawed Dudley Do-Right in a flat-brimmed hat and red shirt chasing claim jumpers on a dogsled, you're way behind the times. What makes Ward unique is his concept of "smart policing," simply defined as police officers working as partners with the people they serve to solve problems in their community. Ward regularly hopscotches around the world to carry his message to police departments in Asia, Europe, and North America. And you will not be astonished that the leadership lessons he has to teach are remarkably similar to my own credo and the lessons learned by other unsung leaders in this book.

When Ward was growing up in the 1970s in Nanaimo, British Columbia, and when he began his career with the Royal Canadian Mounted Police (RCMP) in 1980, police work was an individual affair. Cops decided what the problems were and how they would be resolved. The community's role was to cooperate when asked ("just the facts, ma'am") and then to step aside to let the professionals do their jobs.

The model never felt totally comfortable to Ward, and in practice, it wasn't very effective or efficient either. The police might be zeroing in on burglaries, he explained to me, when community members were griping over the back fence about speeding cars in their neighborhoods or violence in their schools. The institutional arrogance and arm's-length approach to ordinary citizens bothered Ward so much that he actually considered getting out of police work. Luckily, Mounties are encouraged to be creative, adaptive, and flexible, which freed him to test some of his own ideas and kept him from throwing in his bandanna while he was still a lower-ranking member of the force.

Then in 1991, the emerging doctrine of community policing, which had been pioneered across the border in the United States, was officially introduced to the RCMP. Ward Clapham's ideas meshed perfectly with the new philosophy, and he was soon publishing articles, designing workbooks, and giving lectures on the advantages of this partnering philosophy. A series of public service awards followed. Today, in his role as superintendent of the Richmond, British Columbia, RCMP detachment, Ward uses knowledge gleaned from a rich background in policing that spans nearly a quarter century of work in isolated northern Canadian outposts as well as in major cities.

While honing his theory of "smart policing," Ward has also derived some valuable leadership insights that, to my mind, will benefit leaders everywhere. See for yourself.

LESSON: Play by the rules—usually.

What Canadian kids call road hockey is the first station of the cross in ice hockey, the game Canadians of all ages worship as a quasi national religion. Kids play it on streets paved with imaginary ice, using real hockey sticks to hurl balls or rocks at chalk-marked "nets." Since road hockey is ferocious and inexact, loud arguments erupt, prompting neighbors to call the cops and evict the combatants, especially when they play in suburban cul-de-sacs. Prized by players for their lack of traffic, these improvised rinks are also echo chambers that magnify all the shouting and drive some grown-ups nuts.

Ward Clapham, himself a road hockey alumnus, was a brand-new Royal Canadian Mounted policeman when he was first called on to subdue the racket thundering out of a cul-de-sac game in a northern

Alberta town. Speeding to the scene in his shiny police cruiser, dome lights flashing, the young Mountie quickly blocked the street with his car and stepped out, an imposing figure in his broad-brimmed Mountie hat, brown boots, and large pistol. The ragtag players, now scared and silent, studied the ground and waited for the worst.

Instead, Clapham had a mental flash, a reminder that he was a peacekeeper, not a punisher. He decided that befriending noisy kids might help the community more than berating them. So he offered the kids a deal they couldn't refuse: "I can write a ticket for obstructing traffic, or I can play hockey with you."

A relieved grin spread across the young faces, an extra stick was found, and Mountie Clapham played hockey with his much shorter teammates for half an hour. In his enthusiasm, he skimmed off his wide-brimmed hat—good for Ward's hockey game perhaps, but a violation of tight Mountie rules.

The neighbors, peeking from their windows, were outraged. Instead of being punished, the kids were being rewarded, people harrumphed, and the original complainant called the station house again to protest that Clapham had failed to do his duty. His boss chewed him out. He hadn't dealt with the neighbors' complaint. Even worse, he'd taken off his hat in public and cavorted out of uniform, an affront to Mountie dignity.

What the boss didn't understand or much care about was that Ward did more than just play a game. After the play ended, Clapham and the kids talked about all sorts of important topics—girls, drugs, pro hockey, what it's like to be a Mountie, in roughly that order. They bonded. He saw them as potential allies; they saw him as a unique cop, interested in their well-being, not in locking them up. Everyone parted as unexpected friends.

By choosing to speak softly and carry a hockey stick, Ward had grasped the full meaning of his policing responsibilities and given a bunch of rowdy kids a much-needed community role model. "I made a real connection with those kids," he told me. "I found out they were involved in the scout program at school, but didn't have a leader. I felt good when I left, and I told them they could go on playing." Better they should be playing road hockey, he reasoned, than getting into serious trouble—drinking or doing drugs, perhaps, or even considering a burglary for want of anything more interesting to do. Later on, Ward became the group's scoutmaster.

Now a superintendent in the Mounties, Ward makes sure that all his officers carry hockey sticks in their cruisers. The sticks are symbols of his conviction that community policing works best when cops take the lead in reinforcing people's belief that they own their own neighborhoods. Sure, the authorities can literally take over a neighborhood by flooding crime-ridden areas with a slew of hard-nosed cops and tossing bad guys in the slammer. But the positive results will be superficial and temporary—crime will eventually resurface—but the enemies made may last forever. As our troops in Iraq have learned so painfully, the only thing any occupation army really owns is its cache of weapons. Real peace takes long hard work and intense effort by the local populace.

Superintendent Clapham now commands 215 Mounties and 85 support staff in Richmond, British Columbia, and all are encouraged to follow the example he set many years ago on that makeshift hockey rink, working with local people to stop crime before it starts. His standing order—connect with the community—is clear, though not always simple to carry out because it implies that stated rules may sometimes be sacrificed to the overarching cause. And indeed, Clapham's hat story, plus those symbolic hockey sticks, effectively gives his people permission to break the rules whenever it helps them connect with the community.

Let me say, though, that I think this idea is tricky. It's fine for leaders to break rules—if they do it carefully. We often need the slack that permits derring-do in order to inspire our crewmates. But you can't give each sailor the same leeway; you can't run a ship with three hundred free spirits. I found aboard *Benfold* that I had to enforce certain rules without exception. One involved safety (don't endanger lives), another was fiduciary (don't waste taxpayer money). Beyond these inviolate rules, I relied on commander's intent, meaning that I made my policies as clear and strong as possible and allowed my sailors to decide whether our cause overrode a particular rule or regulation. And I did the same when interpreting my own commander's intent, trying to calculate where the overall mission would take precedence over the printed regulations. That's already pushing the envelope in any go-by-the-book military organization.

I am impressed, though, by the RCMP's flexibility in giving Ward such a free hand to establish his own commander's intent. Apparently, his officers feel no undue constraints on reaching out to people and doing whatever it takes to build community ownership. They've come quite a way from the day Ward himself got chewed out for taking off his hat in public.

Ward Clapham seems to have known instinctively, right from the get-go, that effective policing would require some rule bending. His instincts that day in the cul-de-sac were to ignore a couple of rules about hats and kids playing hockey games in order to focus on the larger purpose of being a Mountie. The hat, after all, is just a symbol of police dignity. Wearing it signifies that the cop is on duty, fighting crime and keeping the peace. But if crime fighting and neighborhood building can be better achieved by a hatless cop, then, in my opinion, such symbolism turns petty. Ward proved as much when he won over the youngsters. More to the point, Ward's hockey caper was totally consistent with the Mounties' major objective: crime prevention. His immediate superior just didn't get it; he let his focus on the hat rule obscure the bigger picture.

My own rule on *Benfold* was to separate the hard-and-fast rules from the ambiguous ones. In the first category are things like no alcohol consumption at sea and no violating safety regulations. Never ask your boss about enforcing such rules. Just do it. But ambiguous rules can creep into gray areas that don't promote what you believe are the ship's best interests. That's where leadership comes in. You have to decide what is the commander's true intent.

Get a firm grip on your commander's cause and stick with it, especially when confusion abounds. Like Ward Clapham, I've learned from experience that rules and situational needs are often at odds, partly because the latter change much faster than the former. In theory, for instance, the navy allowed me to hand out only 15 medals a year honoring good performance. I thought that limit was a mistake, preventing me from carrying out my commander's real purpose, which was to build morale and enthusiasm in my crew. So, in my first year on *Benfold,* I handed out 115 medals. I never heard a word from the admiral, which I took as a sign that I had read his intent correctly.

In short, a rule maker can never foresee all the situations with which the rule may intersect in the future. Accordingly, a leader had better identify the rule maker's original purpose and then figure out how to make it fit the situation at hand. (This is precisely what judges do when they interpret the U.S. Constitution's 217-year-old rules to resolve modern disputes.)

Ward Clapham understood that wearing a hat made a Mountie look imposing in hostile territory; he also saw that going hatless served the commander's higher cause of crime prevention. Hats off to Ward Clapham.

LESSON: Mutual respect is vital to team success.

Ward Clapham got his first official taste of leadership as a Mountie when he was given the slow-track job of heading up one of the force's four twelve-member teams within the sixty-member detachment at the Calgary International Airport. Basically, the airport hired the Mounties as security guards; the real policing was done by Calgary city officers— hardly a situation that would make the Mounties feel good about their work. Moreover, Corporal Clapham was the youngest Mountie there and had less seniority than all but one or two of his teammates. Predictably, the older officers saw him as a know-nothing kid, an intruder on their turf. They did their best to ignore Ward, avoiding him the way a small boy ducks a bath.

To turn this surly bunch into a crackerjack team, Ward had first to win their support and, eventually, their respect. He couldn't just order them to salute and smile. These were cops, not robots, and they despised his very presence. "If I tried the standard autocratic way," he told me, "I would go down in flames." Somehow, he had to help them gain enough satisfaction in their work to displace the resentment. They had to enjoy the work they did for him, even if they didn't fully enjoy working with him. It was a tall order.

Creativity and flexibility are prized in the Mountie culture, and Ward made good use of both. First, he became literally unavoidable—he figured the men couldn't dodge him if he never went home. "I worked night shifts and weekends," Ward recalled, "I was there 24/7," demonstrating a commitment to the team.

But Ward knew more was needed, much more. He had to get these people working for him, not against him, as so often happens when you mistake arrogance for leadership. As the boss, it's your job to make tough decisions, but they won't stick unless the team views you as legitimate. How can you persuade them? How can you win respect without losing authority? Ward began experimenting.

Ward vowed never to be found sitting behind his desk. "I needed to be out there with them—on the floor, on the ground, in the cars," he told me. "But I wasn't there to micromanage and drive people crazy by getting in their way. As much as anything, I was there to appreciate their work and show that it was really important—to them as well as to me. I figured that a sense of importance would lead to a sense of ownership, and you know what? It began to happen. Nothing makes you prouder of your work—and yourself—than praise from the boss."

Next, Ward got everyone talking about ways to liven up their jobs and help sharpen the team's performance. He even invited them to see problems through his eyes by playing Corporal Clapham for a day. "I made each of them acting corporal, sitting in my chair, handling the paperwork, setting up the schedule," Ward said, while he observed from afar.

That's an interesting idea I would have liked to try out, but the Mounties are ahead of the U.S. Navy in this regard. Our tradition absolutely forbids anyone but a ship's captain from sitting in the captain's chair. Of course, skippers can still set a Clapham-like example by lending a hand at some difficult job, provided they never lose a captain's requisite aura of command.

Putting his team members in the catbird seat showed Ward not only how well each person could handle a demanding new job, but also how each officer's leadership style affected his colleagues. Watching them act out their versions of Corporal Clapham even helped Ward understand the group's initial standoffishness. Some had resented him because he resembled a previous leader whom they disliked; others balked because he was new and young and they weren't. He started to see where each person was coming from.

For their part, Ward's team members began to appreciate both the new commander's work and his willingness to listen to their opinions. A sense of mutual respect began to reshape the relationship. "It was then," Ward told me, "that I really started to understand the difference between reaching consensus and being autocratic."

Ward, young as he was, had the good sense to shun any display of arrogance or haste. All too often, a new leader will plunge into a troubled situation with gung ho changes that trigger angry inaction. It may well be time to abolish outdated policies and procedures, but to do so without first studying their original intent is to invite failure. Worse, the headstrong reformer is apt to provoke some people to sabotage changes they don't fully understand. Ward knew he had to get involved, listen carefully, respect the group's customs, communicate his plans, and move slowly. He understood that lasting organizational change comes by evolution, not revolution.

As his rapport with his officers grew and his plans took shape, Ward gradually expanded the Mounties' role at Calgary airport. He had no intention of allowing Canada's world-renowned national police to go on playing second fiddle to Calgary's city cops. It was absurd, not to say humiliating, for the Mounties to break up a burglary ring, for instance, and then have to turn the case over to the local police.

To change all that, Ward jettisoned so-called "professional" policing—

just give us the facts, and leave the rest to us—instead, he solicited ideas from the airport community about how police protection should be improved. After organizing a group of airline officials and shop owners to say what kind of security they needed and wanted, he started a new "business watch" procedure to protect the shops and a "lady beware" program to teach women safety precautions for walking to their parked cars.

The airport community applauded, and Ward's Calgary Mounties began to feel needed and appreciated.

But Ward didn't stop there. He went out of his way to help his people develop new skills for future jobs, especially leadership roles. He saw that many of them could easily handle his job; they simply hadn't been coached, mentored, or supported in seeking it. He made it clear that he considered them a talented group with unlimited potential. "I had some officers taking university courses," he told me. "I cut them some slack so they could get to university while they were on duty."

Watching his people grow in skill and satisfaction, Ward felt like a strong father—not a bad way of defining a good leader.

Early one morning, as the sun rose and he headed home after working a twelve-hour shift, Ward felt a sudden burst of love for his job. Everything had finally come together. The team was following through on its investigations with really good paperwork. Every member was taking pride in doing his duty in an unglamorous job. "I was starting to see payback from all my effort," Ward said. "It was great. In my small circle of influence, I had made a real difference. From that point, there was no stopping me."

LESSON: Use informal leaders to help protect your flank.

While still stationed in Edmonton, Ward was assigned to work with the city police in a sting operation aimed at traffickers in stolen goods. Ward and his closest partner, a longtime Edmonton cop, were both well known in the area, which made their undercover role especially risky. Many of the criminals they were trying to trap had met them before in uniform. "They would look at us and ask where it was they knew us from," Ward recalled.

But the duo's casual, offhand manner in a long series of stolen-goods transactions helped them win the thieves' trust. Finally, when the sting produced evidence that the thieves were planning a major operation, Ward and his partner had them arrested.

Prior to trial, while the crooks were being held in the Edmonton jail, they began to compare notes and grew suspicious of their betrayers. No choir boys—some in the ring of thieves had previously been involved in homicides—the talk soon became ugly.

But then, astoundingly, one of the group's informal leaders went to bat for Ward and his partner. Their undercover personas had been so persuasive that this fellow insisted they were good guys who would never squeal. "He actually got into a fight in jail, protecting our reputation," said Ward. And their defender was so convinced, and convincing, that Ward and his partner were fellow criminals, not cops, that other thieves continued to traffic in stolen goods with the pair.

In fact, Ward said, "the first time I met the young man after the investigation was wrapped up, he still would not accept that I was a cop. I showed him my badge and ID and gave him details of how we arrested him every time he committed a crime. But he just would not believe it.

"It's a weird kind of situation, but it gets you thinking about the influence that informal leaders have. This one protected us from all kinds of harm," Ward said, pointing out that word could have spread very quickly without the pair ever knowing their cover had been blown until it was too late.

The truth is, informal leaders can use their influence for ill or good. Throughout history, the best leaders have kept these potential trouble-makers cleanly in sight. One of my favorite examples concerns the legendary Sir Ernest Shackleton, the British explorer who set out in 1914 to claim one of the last remaining prizes in polar exploration: the first crossing by foot of the Antarctic continent. Less than 90 miles from the Antarctic shores, the *Endurance,* on which Shackleton and his crew had sailed the South Atlantic, became entrapped in an ice pack in Antarctica's Weddell Sea. The ship eventually broke apart and the crew was stranded on a drifting ice floe that carried them 350 miles from the nearest land. Their incredible tale of survival might have ended differently had it not been for Shackleton's leadership and his apt understanding of troublemakers.

Known as an incurable optimist and an extraordinary and charismatic leader who always put his men first, Sir Ernest knew the importance of maintaining discipline but still had a generally easygoing manner with his crew. But it was Sir Ernest's astute management of the troublemakers among his crew that may have prevented mayhem in the direst days of the ordeal.

After the ship had broken apart from the battering winds and crushing pressure of the huge, shifting blocks of ice, the crew set up camp some distance away. In his own tent, Sir Ernest collected those who, in the words of a diarist, "he thought wouldn't mix with the others. . . . They were not so easy to get on with." One whom Shackleton was particularly wary of, a man named Frank Hurley, he took pains to consult with and include in important discussions. Hurley, a brilliant photographer who recorded the adventure for posterity, was mentally and physically tough, but Shackleton was unsure of his loyalty. Hurley also had a following among some of the crew members. By keeping him close and tapping his knowledge and expertise, Shackleton helped to ensure that Hurley would not encourage discontent. For Shackleton knew that if he lost his grip on his men, they were probably doomed. Survival depended on every member of the team working together, staying unified.

In the end, the men were saved after Shackleton made an eight-hundred-mile, open-boat crossing to South Georgia Island. Trekking across the mountainous island, he reached a whaling station from which he organized a team to rescue his men. They had endured a twenty-month ordeal on a five-foot-thick sheet of floating ice that held them suspended over the inky depths of the Weddell Sea. At times, the screaming and groaning of the ice plates scraping together must have been maddening. For months at a time, the sun totally disappeared. Through it all, they survived, due in no small part to Shackleton's leadership and his understanding that keeping a potential troublemaker like Hurley on his side was crucial to the group's success.

LESSON: Reach out to strengthen your team.

As a Mountie working with local police all over Canada, Ward Clapham has spent twenty years coping with bruised feelings and turf wars. Local cops naturally resent it when the feds come roaring into town. So Ward, who has an unflinching ability to see the whole picture, can direct his and the team's energy toward cracking the big nut because he has learned how to enlist as many people as possible, including potential rivals and even adversaries, as members of his team.

A prime example involves his assignment to work with the Calgary city police to shut down a major cocaine pipeline from South America. With both the cops and the Mounties working separately to break up the operation, combining minds and muscle was the smart thing to do. What wasn't smart was the tension that developed between the two groups, a potentially fatal flaw if left unchecked.

Calgary was once a wild frontier town in the far western province of Alberta, and as host to the annual Calgary Stampede, the world's biggest rodeo, it still maintains its image as a rugged outpost. Even now, with more than a million in population, Calgarians think of themselves as tough and self-reliant. So do their police—an attitude that smacked the Mounties square in the face when they began the joint effort in 1993. Both sides knew that collaboration was essential to catching the bad guys, but pride and rivalry threatened to derail the investigation—until, that is, Ward Clapham deep-sixed vanity to make sure the kingpin was collared. "If you focus on your relationship," he told me, "the job will get done."

Logistics dictated that the cocaine operation would be run from the Calgary police headquarters, putting the Mounties on unfamiliar turf right from the start. They had to learn a whole new internal operating procedure. Issues of prestige and pecking order instantly caused a rift. "Putting it gently, we were from Venus and they were from Mars," Ward said. In the Mounties, a corporal was a team leader, and could certainly be authorized to spearhead a major drug investigation. But the police "worked in a rank structure where a detective was the almighty. In their minds, he outranked a corporal."

Ward knew that rank is irrelevant. Who cares what your organization calls you or pays you when a hurricane hits or the enemy attacks? Leading means being faster and smarter than anyone else, geared to fighting for what's right. All Ward wanted was to crack the case before the trail faded. But the Calgary cops were unsure about letting the Mounties join their inner circle, and worried that they were trying to take over the investigation. "My guys' opinions were given little credence because we hadn't been there long enough," Ward told me.

The Mounties, who had intelligence sources all across Canada, wanted to bring their insights and information to the partnership. Ward reminded the local cops that "coming in and looking at an old problem in a new way is how problems are solved," but they weren't yet ready to make a leap of faith and accept Ward and his men as integral parts of the team.

Ward staked out the high ground by telling the city police everything he knew and insisting only on reciprocity in return. Even so, the kingpin of the drug ring continued to evade capture. Sure the team could snag small quantities of drugs and their low-level pushers, but the goal was to find the mother lode. Meanwhile, all the petty arrests only seemed to warn the mastermind away from danger.

The project was winding down without any real success. "We weren't able to get the bad guy and we weren't able to get the dope," Ward said. The police tracked the high-level operator to Montreal, where they suspected he was picking up a huge shipment of cocaine to bring to Calgary. But he slipped through their surveillance.

The turning point came when Ward, on a hunch, asked all the Mountie detachments in the province of Ontario, which the dealer would have to cross on his way to Calgary, to go to their local bus stations and board every westbound bus in search of the big dealer. Word came back that the suspect was on a bus headed for Medicine Hat, Alberta, about 180 miles from Calgary.

That's when Ward hit a home run. Rather than keep his mouth shut and let the Mounties get the arrest and all the glory, he immediately tipped off the lead detective on the Calgary police team. Ward knew that a long-term association was at stake here, and if the Mounties were to work successfully with the local cops in the future, they needed to cement a trusting relationship. "[The detective] told me he would kiss me if I wasn't bull-crapping him, and from then on, complete trust was there," Ward told me. "The Calgary team nabbed the guy with all the cocaine, a huge shipment coming to western Canada."

The Mounties cracked a big case and took a dope dealer off the streets, which was the immediate goal. But by letting the Calgary cops get their man, Ward also built a team relationship that thrives to this day—although Ward said he's still waiting for that kiss.

For the life of me, I don't understand how petty rivalries in law enforcement can be allowed to exist, particularly today when it comes to homeland security. All Americans pay for this pettiness in the form of decreased security. The leaders of any government agency charged with protecting us—be it federal, state, or local—should follow Ward's high-minded example.

Wherever he has served, in fact, Ward has found ways to bring would-be competitors or even adversaries onto his team, whether they were rival police forces or angry, disaffected young burglars and vandals. "Get them on the team, whatever it takes," is Ward's philosophy. In the Calgary suburb of Strathmore, Ward used a particularly ingenious wrinkle to widen his circle of crewmates.

The problem was with stores selling cigarettes to minors, a practice the Canadian government was attacking by sending undercover operators to expose the culprits and then taking them to court, where they were fined. Ward had a different idea, and after clearing it with

Canada's health and welfare officials, he went to court one day and asked the judge to suspend charges against the store owners while he tried a new approach. The judge agreed.

Ward's solution was an antismoking campaign, starting with an education session for employees of the offending stores. Since the store owners were eager to avoid the looming fines, it was standing room only. In the end, store owners and employees alike signed on to Ward's team.

The program was so effective that when the feds ran another sting operation, they found no violations at all. Parents and school officials were happy. And Darryl Badard, the Mountie that Ward had assigned to run the operation, got a special citation from the Canadian Cancer Society.

Later in his career, when Ward had become an inspector and was working in his hometown, Nanaimo, on Vancouver Island, he took the same tack with bar owners whose happy hours were spilling crowds of belligerent drunks into the streets. Ward enlisted the bar owners in "social contracts" that recognized the problems caused by predatory pricing and serving inebriated people, and effectively created a cease-fire in the happy-hour war. Any community can do the same with similar issues, he believes; it's just a matter of asking people to take responsibility for the problem they themselves are causing.

LESSON: Challenge yourself, and grow.

After his triumph with the drug team in Calgary, Ward Clapham was one of the Mounties' bright stars; he could have picked any posting he wanted, including a cushy job as commander in a quiet, orderly town near a military base. Instead, he chose a hellhole everyone else shunned, a town so bleak and violent that the RCMP had to promise short tours of duty and subsequent plum assignments to persuade officers to serve there at all.

The name of this hellhole was, fittingly enough, Faust (unlike that of the magician of German legend who enters into a compact with the devil, this name is pronounced "fost," which rhymes with *frost*). Ward himself made a Faustian bargain, but it turned the traditional meaning on its head. Rather than taking the job for present gain without regard for future consequences, Ward saw the present torture as an opportunity for future gain.

His fellow Mounties all thought he was crazy, Ward told me years later. "But I wanted the hardest job—to take the challenge and push it." It was his own ship, he explained: "I had a circle of influence where I could put everything into play from A to Z, and the buck stopped with me."

Faust Detachment covers a collection of hamlets on the shore of Lesser Slave Lake in the wilds of Alberta. The inhabitants of the actual hamlet of Faust were mainly what Canadians now call First Nations people, Amerindians who scratched a basic living from fishing and mink farming and were plagued by an inordinate amount of drug and alcohol addiction, domestic abuse, and violent crime.

Driving into town for the first time in 1994, Ward steered around gaping potholes as his wife, clutching their baby boy, no doubt wondered what her husband had gotten them into. "My wife didn't say a word," Ward recalled. "She was a good trooper, but she was swallowing quite heavily there." Choking is probably more like it, as the young mother gazed through the car window at abandoned houses with shattered windowpanes—shacks, really—in rubble-strewn lots. They passed an empty school with boarded-up windows that reflected not the gaily colored creations of happy youngsters in a nurturing environment but the hard reality of abject poverty.

Should Ward and his wife wish to stroll down one of Faust's rutted streets, they had to carry a can of bear spray to fend off potential attacks by grizzlies and packs of wild dogs. Interbred with wolves and coyotes, the dogs snarled and growled menacingly as the couple made their way along the dreary streets. The residents were no more welcoming. Ward's friendly waves drew rigid, hostile stares as he drove around town. The citizens of Faust saw the Mounties as hunters and themselves as the prey.

As for his work, Ward had a team of only four officers and an office manager to police a community of three thousand that had Alberta's third-highest per capita crime rate. He and his crew worked virtually nonstop, taking little time off. "I was wildly busy," Ward remembered, "and the officers were going night and day." There were so many calls that they had to perform a risky kind of triage, deciding which calls might be ignored safely. It was a harrowing situation that called for a new kind of leadership, and Ward Clapham set out to deliver it. It was in Faust that Ward's ideas and style of leadership finally jelled into a technique that engages and motivates his officers to become part of the communities they serve, and in so doing, to achieve uncommon results.

One of the first, and most critical, things Ward did in Faust was to devise an inside-out approach to leadership that helped him to prioritize more than just the problems on the job. He wisely learned to first sort out what was most important for him personally, for his family, and then for his team. "If I'm no good, then I'm not going to be any good to anyone else," he realized, "and if my family needed a week to settle in, I had to get my affairs in order at home. Then [came] the new reality of the team."

In typical Ward Clapham fashion, he wanted to move at a measured pace that would allow him to honor the team's customs while getting to know his people individually and become involved in their lives. All of that was necessary, he knew, before he could communicate his own ideas effectively and move his team in the direction he wanted it to go. Any leader who expects to impose his will from on high and then win confidence without first understanding who he's dealing with is likely to stumble. As part of Ward's inside-out approach, he held meetings, conversed one on one to get acquainted, went out for coffee with his people, and constantly watched and listened to understand their concerns, goals, and issues.

Although he had recently been promoted, Ward asked his team to address him not as Sergeant Clapham but by his first name. He had no intention of being seen as the commander or the boss, he told me. Rather, he saw himself as the first among equals—"detachment enabler" was the title he bestowed on himself. "That raised some eyebrows, I can tell you," he chuckled. Next he announced that from then on, three kinds of decisions would be made: consensus decisions, in which everyone had to agree; democratic decisions, reached by a vote; and autocratic orders, which he had to give—but only, he promised, after consulting with his team and giving serious consideration to their opinions.

As for day-to-day operations, Ward jettisoned one of his predecessor's customs in short order. Rather than work the day shift, Monday through Friday, mainly doing paperwork at his desk, Ward followed the team's urging and worked every other weekend, including Friday and Saturday nights. He also made it a point to go out on patrol with his men to get a bird's-eye view of what they were up against. The changes at the top opened up the schedule for the whole detachment, and gave the officers some weekend time off. "Morale skyrocketed almost immediately," said Ward. He gained "instant credibility [because] they were getting support, and there were more boots on the street." The schedule changes also gave the boss the chance to lead by example, engaging and coaching his men in real situations and showing them how to deal with the people and problems of Faust.

Working alongside his officers in Faust, it didn't take Ward long to figure out that manpower was not the only thing lacking. The detachment needed more and better equipment—like four-wheel-drive patrol cars to handle unplowed back roads in forty-below weather, all-terrain vehicles and snowmobiles to patrol remote trails, a boat to answer calls on the lake. Thanks to the prestige he had built in Calgary, he got them.

The results were dramatic. With cell phones in all the cars, for instance, communication improved markedly. Showing up at a domestic dispute, an officer could phone the house to appraise the situation. If a woman said, "Don't come in; he's got a knife," the officer could ask to speak directly to the man and warn him of the consequences of his actions.

Most important, Ward came to understand the real meaning of

community policing. The professional model of police work largely re-
stricts cops to handling problems and criminals. They are on a first-
name basis with every criminal in town, but seldom meet the
upstanding, hardworking citizens or see the positive activities that
make up 99 percent of a town's day-to-day life. By the same token, the
townspeople view the cops as stern enforcers or, sometimes, as preda-
tors. "You only come to arrest Mommy and Daddy," was what one
small boy told Ward.

By contrast, community policing begins with consulting the community, discussing its real goals and problems, and trying to find a permanent solution instead of merely tossing a problem in jail for a while.
Ward had his officers go out in civilian clothes to set up discussion
groups in each of Faust's hamlets, visit churches and schools, and have
coffee with respected leaders in each community.

One Mountie, Ron Smith, was a regular luncher at a community
school, where he became an idol and role model for the kids—and
Ward subsidized the connection by paying for Smith's lunches.

The officers learned, Ward said, that "these people are no different
from you and me. They are just accustomed to a different lifestyle."
One lesson of community policing, he explained, is that "you aren't
there to judge, but to support and understand." As they learned, the
cops became more tolerant. Rather than throw the book at a couple
having a domestic dispute, for instance, they would try to make peace.

In time, the Mounties were seen as friends—so much so that Ward
printed up "cop cards," like baseball trading cards, for each of his officers. They handed them out to anyone who had done a good deed or
shown friendship. The cards became wildly popular. The favorite
Mountie was Perry Cardinal, himself a First Nations Canadian. Children and grown-ups alike cherished their Perry Cardinal cards.

A cop card may even have saved a Mountie's life. Answering a call
about a man wielding a gun, two officers arrived to find a guy sprawled
on the ground, evidently knocked unconscious by a club lying across
his shoulders. They arrested the fellow who had clubbed the man on
the ground, but turned him loose when he explained that the "victim"

was actually the gunman who had been planning to shoot them both. The gunman had put in the call himself, hoping to lure them to their deaths. The Good Samaritan, it turned out, felt kindly toward the Mounties because an officer had given him a ride home—and handed him a cop card. The cards were a good deal more than a public relations gimmick, Ward said—they were bridge builders to the community.

In the end, both the Mounties and Faust underwent a sea change, all because Ward Clapham "wanted the hardest job—to take the challenge and push it." The cops became part of the community, tolerant of petty misdemeanors but serious about making it a better place to live. The citizens of Faust gained pride and self-respect, and they began to think big thoughts of their own. "Some of the First Nations communities set up their own police service, and were looking at self-government," Ward told me.

LESSON: Start small, and build from there.

Ward Clapham learned a good many lessons in training and using his team of Mounties in Faust, and one of them was to start small—to begin with tasks that are relatively easy, use them to build trust and confidence both inside the team and with the community, and move on from there to harder problems.

One early problem was the bar at the Faust Hotel, a dive notorious for its wild drinking and violent fights. Here was a problem that cried out for a solution, but no matter what happened, the bar staff never called the Mounties. Ward and his officers would hear after the fact that someone had sauntered in with a gun and shot up the place. Or they would see for themselves shards of glass on the sidewalk from beer bottles smashed for use as weapons.

Reluctant to enter the bar without being called—"we would have been the victims," Ward told me—the officers cautiously got to know the staff and some of the customers. Then Ward started venturing inside. "I would go in, by myself or with someone else, and I'd go up to the bartender and order a ginger ale or a Coke, and I'd sit down at one of the bar tables and chat," Ward said. "They were drinking beer and I'd have my pop, and we'd chat, laugh, and talk about whatever the issues were." On Friday night, karaoke night, Ward would turn up in uniform and sing; his crowd-pleaser was "I Fought the Law, and the Law Won."

Ward has an edge on me there. I had regular karaoke nights on *Benfold,* when everybody got up and sang—officers, chiefs, shipmates, everyone but me. The captain was not authorized to sing because the captain didn't know how to sing.

As the drinkers in the hotel bar got to know him, Ward could comfortably advise someone who was in his cups, "Now look, Johnny, your car's out front, but don't be driving home tonight. I'll give you a ride home." He would return at closing time and keep the promise, much preferring to escort a Faustian home rather than having to fill out the paperwork to process a drunk driver or, worse yet, clean up an accident scene.

That was proof to Faust that the Mounties were part of the community, that they were human, and that they meant what they said— all of which helped the mission along. But it also paved the way for more serious dialogue at the bar. "Now I could tell them that we had zero tolerance for spousal assault, and if they crossed the line, they would be going down hard—that I would throw the last ounce of the law at them," Ward explained. The real message was beginning to get through.

LESSON: Throw problems back to your people.

A crisis erupted for the Mounties of Faust when the RCMP cut the wages of prison guards to nine dollars an hour. All of the guards quit, correctly reasoning that they could live better on unemployment or other social assistance programs. Consequently, with no one to ride herd on the prisoners, Ward and his team couldn't put anyone in jail. Where once the Faust Detachment had hundreds of prisoners locked up, most of them drunks or people being held on misdemeanor charges, now Ward and his team could detain only a handful. Making a virtue of necessity, he took a calculated risk and turned the drunks loose, then handed the problem over to the community.

When someone called the Mounties asking them to arrest a drunken spouse, for example, the officers explained they could no longer jail the offender, so the caller had to figure out a way to solve the problem. Oftentimes, other Faustians—friends or relatives of the offender, perhaps even the caller herself—had played a part in aiding and abetting the drinking. Might they accept some of the responsibility for the result? the Mounties asked. Sometimes, Ward would point out that the only available jail space was in the next town. Would the caller prefer that he leave the community short of police staff for two hours to drive a drunk to jail?

To be sure, Ward was playing a risky game. Any one of those cases could have turned violent and done serious damage, exposing the Mounties not only to legal liability but a major loss of credibility and respect. But having earlier made it his business to get to know the community, and having worked to engage its people to participate in their own policing, the risk Ward took was a calculated one. He believed he had acquired enough knowledge about Faust's citizens to correctly gauge the probabilities. In the end, "We gave the community ownership not only of drunks, but of the whole alcohol problem, and of being responsible and working with us."

I learned the same lesson years ago on *Benfold:* If you can't solve a problem, throw it back to the person who brought it. Nine times out of ten, they will handle it—and grow in the process.

LESSON: Help your team members grow.

As he did in all his postings, Ward took pains to provide positive feedback for his team in Faust. "It doesn't take anything to tell someone he's doing a great job," he said. He also spent time and effort making sure that each member of his team was preparing for the next step on the career ladder, whatever that might be. "I've sat down with every person I ever worked with," he said, "and asked them where they were, where they wanted to go, and then how should we get to that point." As the officers told him their goals, he showed them what he expected of them. Then, he said, "We developed a road map."

He discovered, for instance, that one of his Mounties, Peter Sandziuk, wanted to take a specialized course in spotting drug traffickers transporting drugs along the highway through Alberta. To free him up for the ten-day absence, Ward volunteered to work his shift and take on his investigations—a major addition to Ward's own job as sergeant. It was an eye-opener, he said. "It brought me back down to the reality of what my people were facing day in and day out."

Determined to milk every advantage from Sandziuk's experience, Ward asked him on his return to teach the whole team what he had learned. It's important, Ward believes, for anyone attending a course or workshop to share their newfound knowledge and skills. Remember the old saying "To teach is to learn twice"? Peer teaching is both cost-effective and enormously beneficial to your staff. For one thing, it increases productivity; for another, it deepens the understanding of the peer teacher to look at the material from a different angle.

The drug-busting technique Sandziuk learned mainly involves close observation of suspicious vehicular traffic. Officers making a routine traffic stop are taught to be especially mindful of incongruous behavior by drivers and passengers. Drug traffickers may go to great lengths to fit in to their environment. It's the officer's job to look past the obvious for clues and evidence. "It's the indicators that tweak your sense that maybe something is going on," Ward said. In general, the officers are taught to use an educated sixth sense about suspicious activities and to follow up effectively. An officer who's been through the program doesn't rush a traffic stop, said Ward. "We take time to interact and we use our senses."

Although Ward wholeheartedly supported Sandziuk's desire to attend the course, I don't think he ever imagined just how big and fast the payoff might be. Less than a week after his return, out in the boondocks of northern Alberta, Peter Sandziuk stopped a huge shipment of marijuana on its way to the Northwest Territories. It was a major coup for the detachment and for Ward, and it reinforced his determination to help his people keep growing. "All I had to do was to believe in my people," he said. "It was a reminder to me every day."

LESSON: Solve the real problem.

Too often, according to Ward Clapham, police work is just putting Band-Aids on festering problems that come back time and again to plague a community. Locking up drunks, for instance, does nothing to keep them from getting drunk again. What's needed is to get them, their families, and the whole community to accept responsibility for the problem. In Faust, Ward had a similar epiphany about the chronic problem of youthful crime.

It was out of control, he said. Young people would roam the community all night, vandalizing and burgling; calls for help in the small hours were exhausting the Mounties and running up overtime. When Ward asked some youngsters with whom he had forged a bond why they were doing this to him, their cheeky reply was: "Why are you doing this to us?" Curbing his instinctive retort that *he* wasn't the one committing crimes, Ward recognized that in a real sense these were his clients, so he had to find a way to understand them. After some serious thought, he came to see that the root cause was boredom—these kids had nothing else to do.

That's when Ward decided to ask a revolutionary question: what would they like to do? Play basketball, they answered. Ward anointed one kid as the project leader. "He was to get together a team of boys, and I was to get them the equipment and put up a basketball hoop," Ward said. The hoop went up on a slab of concrete at the local school-yard, after which Ward made the rounds of all the hamlets in Faust, offering the same deal to each group of kids. Teams sprang up everywhere. When residents complained about the noise of games at 2:00 A.M., Ward commiserated but then reminded them of what the kids had been doing at 2:00 A.M. *before* they began playing basketball—drinking, breaking into stores, damaging property.

In Ward's own part of town, the only available piece of pavement was the Mountie detachment's parking lot. So he closed the lot to visitors and turned it into a playground, complete with basketball hoops, hockey nets, and other equipment bought with funds raised in the community. Ward also told his Mounties to file and forget their investigative folders on the kids. Their new job was to play basketball and hockey with the young citizens of Faust. He sent his officers out into the community to round up the kids. "I don't care how you get them here," he instructed, "just round 'em up." And that's what the officers did. As Ward admits, some who showed up were a little unwilling at first. He also arranged for a supply of water and food, basically an outdoor concession stand, at the playground, and even rented a Porta Potti for the kids to use.

When Ward sent out a press release about the Porta Potti to the local papers, it went by mistake to national media as well. Editors all over Canada had fun with the story—MOUNTIES TO THE OUTHOUSE and MOUNTIES GET THEIR JOHN read typical headlines. But the real story came through loud and clear: chasing delinquent kids and hauling them into court wasn't working, so we're trying something different.

Still, Ward was worried. Using taxpayers' money to provide a toilet for juvenile delinquents probably broke every rule in sight.

When Ward's commanding officer telephoned him, he momentarily envisioned his job going down the, well, toilet and wondered if he could find a job with the city police in Victoria. But what he heard from his CO was: "I am so proud of you. How can I help you? What more can I do? What can we here at headquarters do to support and help you? This is the best thing. . . ." Ward says they probably heard his sigh of relief all the way to Manitoba.

Juvenile crime in Faust dropped to almost zero that summer, and Ward's overtime budget was back under control. Officers and kids alike were having fun. And when one boy did commit a burglary, the others turned him in to the Mounties. "They were mad and upset," Ward explained. "They felt they could lose everything because this guy had done something stupid."

Oh, and when Ward caught a boy stealing bread, he didn't let it jeopardize the activities program. This time, he correctly guessed that the root problem was that the kid was hungry. The solution: "We started feeding him."

LESSON: Look after your people first.

When Ward Clapham arrived to take charge of the RCMP station in Richmond, he found a smelly warren of shabby rooms, sagging furniture, and obsolete computers. His own office was equally forgettable— except for the garish pink chair behind the desk. Pink is hardly the color for a police commander's throne. In his situation, eager to make the right impression, you and I instantly would have flung the thing out the door. I would have stood behind my desk for a month, if necessary, to avoid being seen in a pink chair.

Not Ward Clapham. He's a leader of a different hue.

His new colleagues encouraged him to get a different chair, but Ward refused. Until they all had proper furniture and equipment, he insisted, he was going to stick with the office he'd inherited. "I wasn't going to spend a dime of public money until all my people were happy," Ward told me. And he set about making the phone calls and sending the e-mails to get them the workstations, chairs, and computers "they deserved," as he put it.

Some months later, he got to work early one morning and found that the pink chair was missing. In its place was what Ward described as a "brand-new, leather, high-back, state-of-the-art king chair." He immediately rolled it right out into the hallway and informed an aide that he wanted his pink chair back.

She shook her head. "Ward, you don't get it. Everybody else now has everything we need. It's your turn."

Ward did finally get it: This king chair was "like a badge of honor that they wanted me to have," he said, "and it meant a lot to them." He gladly kissed the pink chair good-bye.

That was a good illustration of leadership. As the new superintendent, Ward had known all eyes would be on him for clues as to the kind of boss he would be. He responded by using something concrete, the pink chair, to show his team that their needs came before his own. In this age when successful people are encouraged at every turn to flaunt their achievements—"You've earned it," the ads proclaim—Ward believes it's critically important for a leader to flip the message so that the team members who make your success possible are rewarded first.

Ward recalls a meeting he had with "a nice, smart, senior government official," during which he talked about how important it was to him to look after his people. "Where do you find the time?" she asked. "Your approach simply wouldn't work for us because we are too busy doing more important things."

Ward was dumbfounded. "I must have sat there for five seconds without saying anything, staring at her," he recalled. "Finally, I said, 'Where do I *not* find the time? This is job one. You have to know your people are your most valuable asset and that they're the ones who deliver the goods. It's got to be a two-way street.'"

Teams take real ownership of their jobs, ready to break new ground and go for broke, when they respect and identify with their leader and their leader's goals. To win that respect, leaders have to demonstrate their own commitment to the well-being and morale of their troops.

By the time he had finished with the government official, Ward added, she was a convert: "Even though she was shaking her head sideways, I could tell she was saying, 'I get it.'"

LESSON: To lead your team, be part of it.

When Ward Clapham went to Strathmore in the fall of 1996, he was promoted to staff sergeant leading a team of fifteen officers. He was still getting acquainted when one day, sitting at his desk, he heard the dispatcher call in a car from patrol because there was no one in the office to fingerprint a suspect—a messy, time-consuming job that most Mounties detest. Ward immediately countermanded the call and said he would do the job himself. He explained, "I needed them out there doing what they do best, and why shouldn't I do it when I'm available? It wasn't a big deal. And actually it turned out that the guy I was fingerprinting was pretty cool. I learned a lot about the community from picking his brain as we went through the exercise."

What Ward didn't know was that he was sending shock waves through his detachment, which couldn't believe that a lofty staff sergeant would literally dirty his hands with drudge work. It was the beginning of a new kind of team in Strathmore, one in which the relationship between the leader and his troops was firmly grounded in trust and mutual respect.

Not long after, having gone out on patrol with one of his officers in an effort to learn about the community, Ward reinforced the team's first impression when he volunteered to handle a drunk driver. You might think—or at least his officers probably did—that the chief might blow it. After all, at this point Ward was a sixteen-year veteran who, for several of those years, had been heading up detachments, not spending the bulk of his time in day-to-day police work. But like the experienced professional that he is, Ward smoothly pulled the driver off the road and out of his car. He administered a sobriety test, cautioned the guy about his rights, arrested him, and, back at the station house, he gave the suspect a Breathalyzer test—all without a hitch. Later, at a sobriety-checking roadblock on the Trans-Canada Highway, Ward, acting on a hunch, pulled a car out of the line and discovered that, sure enough, the driver was impaired.

What Ward was proving was that he wasn't just brass; he was also a very good cop.

Ward wanted to make his office a friendly place, but his officers tended to assume that when they got called in, they must have done something wrong. So he made a point of calling people in from patrol, using the radio so everyone would know, and then delivering a compliment on a job well done. (On board *Benfold,* I was fond of using the

PA system in exactly the same way.) It didn't take long before the buzz in the Strathmore Detachment was all about the generous praise handed out by the staff sergeant. Pretty soon Ward's office lost its stigma. Instead, it became the coveted place to be.

But the day Ward came to work and found his office furnishings piled in the bull pen, he knew he had just received a grand compliment. "It was huge," he said. "It was the sign that I had been accepted. They believed and trusted me and were willing to follow me." Relishing his acceptance, Ward decided to keep his office in the bull pen. "From there I was able to get the team to buy into the real initiatives that needed to move forward," he told me.

Later in his career, when Ward was an inspector on Vancouver Island, he was made commander of the island's emergency response team—the equivalent of a SWAT team in the United States. But he had no experience in the work. Typically, Ward decided to lead from the front, taking part in every training exercise his troops went on. "I wasn't going to try and buffalo my way around these officers who knew their stuff inside out," he said. "Instead, I decided to get involved from the ground up."

As part of that process, Ward went to a three-day regional exercise in bush tracking, the arduous business of locating and arresting suspects hiding in dense wilderness. It amounts to jungle warfare, including techniques of tracking, avoiding booby traps and ambushes, using disabling gas, managing police dogs, setting up night patrols, and the like. It was hard work and the weather was wretched, cold and rainy. Ward went as a team member, and his officers kept the secret that he was really the commander until the last day of the exercise. Then they introduced him to the other teams, who were as impressed as they were incredulous that an inspector would put himself through such an ordeal. "I did it for the right reasons," Ward told me, a bit sheepishly, "but I have to say that it spread like wildfire all through the RCMP. I was known as the ops commander who could get down and dirty with the guys."

LESSON: Stay focused on the real goal.

When Ward Clapham took over as head of the SWAT team on Vancouver Island, he soon realized he had a problem: His "ninjas"—the black-clad commandos who rescue hostages, execute very risky arrests of holed-up fugitives, raid drug rings, and the like—and his crisis interveners and hostage negotiators weren't meshing as smoothly as they should have been. All train for the same goal, a peaceful resolution, but their approaches can sometimes seem at odds. What ninjas want to do, Ward told me, is throw their concussion grenades into a house and charge in after them, "because this is what they are trained to do and they are mostly triple-A personalities. That is just who they are." The negotiators are patient, nonthreatening people whose goal is to avoid all violence. However, the negotiators had to understand that if the ninjas were called in, they needed as much data as possible about the situation. It was up to the negotiators to get it.

It took some time, Ward said, but he was able to get the two groups together for joint training in simulated crisis situations, and they began to see each other's viewpoints. It paid off in the case of a man in Duncan, a small town in the Cowichan Valley on the island's east coast, who had barricaded himself in a house, threatening suicide. Since no one else was in danger, Ward felt that time was on his side. "As far as I was concerned, we could be there for a month," rotating the teams until the man either went through with his threat or gave up. Rushing in would expose the ninjas to danger, and they could injure the man or trigger his suicide. "If he's trying to take his own life, we aren't trying to accelerate that," Ward told me dryly.

Thanks to their training, the ninjas understood that their role was to keep things under control for the negotiators. The negotiators were now helping the ninjas too. When the man finally decided to come out, the negotiators got him to leave through a designated door and lie down quietly so that the ninjas could approach him safely, handcuff him, and take him into custody. The nonviolent outcome was a huge success for both parts of the team, Ward told me. The mission was accomplished in the best possible fashion—without a drop of blood being spilled.

A key part of any such crisis operation is the postaction debriefing, which in turn feeds advance planning for the next similar situation. On *Benfold*, we called this process the after action review, or AAR. After every major event or maneuver, all those involved got together and critiqued it. A critical piece of the process was the lack of rank. Everyone was open to criticism, even me.

Ward also spared no one, including himself, in his team's debriefings. After a raid on a marijuana-growing operation, for instance, Ward faulted himself at the debriefing for not taking account of a nearby school. The school had been letting out just as the black-clad assault team, toting machine guns and wearing helmets and bulletproof vests, arrived, frightening the children into nightmares.

Chastened by the experience and discussing where he had gone wrong in the subsequent debriefing, Ward changed the team's procedures to make sure nothing like that happened again. In a similar operation later, Ward notified the school in advance, and the children were kept inside until the raid was over. Similar contingency plans were made for other situations. When surveillance of a drug ring indicated there were children on the scene, the team took a more low-key approach and softened its entry to the house, making the situation as unthreatening as possible for the children while still assuring that the raid was successful.

But if a team is to be kept together and in focus, Ward believes, both training and debriefing must be totally transparent, candid, and consensual. "When we debrief, when we train, all rank is left at the door," he told me. "Everybody is equal, and everybody's opinion matters. We all learn from each other. I make the point that I'm never called by my rank; my name is Ward." But it's equally important that once a decision is made, everyone must get behind it. "You can agree to disagree agreeably, whatever it takes," he said. "But when you walk out, you have to have a united voice."

LESSON: Show people that you care.

Ward Clapham is, in my opinion, one of the shrewdest Mounties in Canadian history. He is also a true believer in the broken-window theory of police work. The theory holds that if you simply ignore a broken window in a house, a bus scrawled with graffiti, or similar instances of vandalism, it conveys the message that nobody's in charge and nobody cares. That, in turn, encourages further vandalism.

For Ward, there is a larger message here. In all lines of work, from business to policing to seafaring, it pays to let people know that someone is in charge, that someone cares. "In the information age," he said, "there is a rebellion against automation," such as the automated telephone-response system where you never get to speak to a real person no matter how many buttons you push. "People want and deserve real human interaction," Ward asserted.

To that end, he has inspired his officers to provide their own personal touch when dealing with crime victims. When there is a break-in, for example, Ward's officers take down the facts and offer the victim some tips on how to make the house more secure—standard police procedure. What isn't standard is the officers' follow-up response. A week later, they drop by the house again to report on what's been happening with the case and to find out if there has been any further trouble. They leave a card and tell householders to call if they need anything.

"After the people fall off their chairs because they can't believe what you've done," Ward said, "they have a changed attitude toward the police. They become fans who will help us and cooperate with us in ways they never would have before."

Ward, who doesn't let himself off the hook when it comes to personal interaction, has binders full of the business cards of people he has met in the course of his work. Once a week he reaches into the binders, pulls out several cards, and calls the people named. "I reintroduce myself," he said, "and ask if there's anything I can do to help them.

They're blown away. It changes the way they think about me and my people."

During a call to the leader of a crime-prevention association, Ward discovered that the group needed a senior police person to champion their work. Would he promote them at a meeting? Of course, Ward replied. It's all part of his interaction with the people he serves—"part of building up the human connection, of letting people know that there is a real person here who cares," he told me.

In my own experience as a leader, few things cement a relationship like your willingness to take the extra step, to touch base, to let the other person know that you are concerned about him or her. Even if the window is perfectly intact, so to speak, a follow-up call to a client or a customer can make all the difference in your ongoing relationship.

LESSON: Never put down your people.

How many times has this happened to you? You're in a brainstorming session with lots of people firing smart ideas. But when you toss one out for discussion, the leader says something like, "No, that doesn't make any sense," or "Does anybody else have any ideas?" Nothing squelches creativity and the free flow of ideas like an insensitive manager.

Ward Clapham, who actively seeks out the ideas of his officers and is particularly sensitive to keeping them flowing freely, would never do that to his people. "Not when I'm practically begging them to think big, be creative, find new ways to make our policing better," he said. "The one thing I don't want is for any of them to feel turned off, as if their ideas were foolish. Put-downs are poison. I can't think of a faster way to create a deadly enemy than to laugh off someone's earnest idea in public."

It's no easy task to get your people thinking creatively in the first place. When they do overcome apathy or custom, the result can be thrilling. Sometimes you feel like a backpacker who has just managed to spark a fire with damp matches. You never want to douse the flame, to throw away new possibilities by belittling anybody's sincere suggestion, even if it's not exactly a winner.

But how do you deal with the bad ideas that come your way along with the good? To start, he told me, you manage your people's expectations by defining what kind of suggestions are appropriate. They won't propose installing, say, a cotton-candy machine because you've made it clear that's not the kind of idea you're soliciting. "If something really frivolous like that actually came up," Ward remarked, "I would probably say, 'Yes, that's an interesting idea, but the reason why we can't do it is such-and-such.'" Or he might counter a bad idea on a serious topic by saying that he's putting it on his wish list of things to do—he'll keep it in mind, but it will be toward the bottom of his list. "They're okay with that," he said. "It doesn't shut them down."

Another technique Ward uses to avoid hurt feelings while also increasing staff cohesion is to give each of his units a special budget for carrying out new ideas. "I authorize them to decide whether an idea will fly or not," he said. It turns out that the officers know very well which ideas are worth pursuing. The money doesn't get wasted. At the same time, the idea originator doesn't get upset if his inspiration fizzles. He knows it got a fair hearing by a jury of his peers who will continue to value him as a fellow team member, with all rights intact. Result: an ever freer exchange of ideas.

LESSON: Stay close to your people.

"No news is good news" may be true for a fire chief, but such occasions are rare in the life of most other successful leaders. Sitting behind your desk, you may want to believe that because there are no obvious problems, none exist—but in your heart of hearts, you know better. In any organization bad things are always just around the corner. Your job as a leader is to maintain direct communication with your troops so you can keep the problems to a minimum. You have to seek out, identify, and repair anything that threatens to undermine your team's dedication.

Ward Clapham keeps in touch by moving constantly around his offices, his officers' beats, and his community. He pops in unannounced at team meetings, or joins people eating lunch in the cafeteria, or tags along when some of his officers attend weekend police leadership conferences. When he finds something wrong, large or small, he pounces on it. More than anything, Ward wants his officers to keep on feeling the pride that inspires their enthusiasm and innovation.

Ward told me about the day he went for a run at lunchtime (an infrequent event), and then showered in the detachment's locker room. He "blew a gasket" when he discovered that all the soap dispensers were empty. "My people go around in flak jackets with twenty-five pounds of gear, working twelve-hour shifts in the heat and the rain, and there was no soap in their showers. So I took out my credit card, marched down in full uniform to the local grocery, and bought out their supply of soap.

"It's about the little things," he continued—the small, annoying, everyday frustrations that can build resentment and get between team members and their leader, or between them and their jobs. "To connect with people without filtering is a real challenge," Ward added.

One of his favorite techniques is the daily morning meeting at which officers are urged to speak their minds about their assignments and working conditions. "Everybody's rank is left at the door," he said. At one session, for example, someone raised a problem regarding allocation of manpower within the detachment; Ward proposed a solution, and a sergeant disagreed. "He countered my opinion," Ward said. "His suggestion to move resources around was totally different from mine, but he was right. I told him so and commended him for speaking out about it."

That's exactly the kind of straightforward talk that opens people up and encourages shared confidences. It makes it possible for leaders to find out what's really going on—and to solve small problems before they fester and grow into big ones.

During one of Ward's strolls around the office, as he stopped people to ask how they were doing and whether or not they were encountering any problems, an officer mentioned that he and his fellows had no computers. Ward was aghast. "The offices were hardwired and good to go," he recalled, "but there was no equipment." He immediately phoned his information technology staff. It turned out the computers were in-house, but still sitting in their boxes. Within minutes they were on the way as Ward scrambled around moving furniture and pulling out dropped wires. "It was just a mix-up in communication," he said, "but it took the boss walking by to find out about it."

When Ward talks about his walking-around experiences, he always adds that they are essential not just to support intelligent management of his unit, but as morale builders. People who are convinced the boss cares about them will themselves care, in turn, about performing better and earning the boss's greater approval. But this ideal outcome depends on the leader's going directly to team members; he must find out enough to prove that he really cares and isn't just another empty suit that can't be trusted.

Ward's approach is bearing fruit. The Richmond Detachment has gone from having one of the worst attraction and retention rates in the RCMP to one of the best. People are lining up to transfer into the detachment, Ward told me. "Our promotion rate is double the RCMP average and our people are now fully engaged in our new direction of policing."

An honest look at Ward's philosophy and the way he carries it out is enough to convince anyone who might be wondering why the Richmond unit has the best morale within the RCMP.

LESSON: When you know you're right, stick to your guns.

At Strathmore, Ward Clapham was determined to replicate his success with the young people of Faust. To that end, he assigned each of his Mounties to a local school, charging the officers with cooking up ways to bond with the students. Soon some of his officers came back complaining that they couldn't seem to reach the kids. Maybe the kids were put off by officers in uniform, or maybe the officers weren't able to spend enough time to win them over. Whatever the reasons for the shaky start, Ward believed strongly in the concept and wasn't about to be deterred.

Somehow he wangled eight season tickets to home games of the Calgary Flames hockey team. In hockey-obsessed Canada, few kids would pass up a chance like this, no matter how they might feel about the Mounties. The officers would take turns using the tickets and would pick seven students to accompany them to the games, based on any criteria the officers chose—kids determined to be at risk, or someone who had done a good deed or won a contest, or maybe just some nice average kid who didn't make noise and got overlooked because of it. Each officer decided to use different criteria in the Onside Program, so named by Ward because it aimed to keep kids on the right side of the law. ("Onside" is a hockey term that means a player is legally in position to receive the puck.)

The program was a success all around. The kids loved it and so did the Mounties. And Ward, who had no doubt that his team was helping the kids, gave the effort his wholehearted—and whole-wallet—support. Could the Mounties take kids to the games in a police car? Sure. Could they be reimbursed for parking at the stadium? Absolutely. Money to buy the kids popcorn and soda? Ward provided it. Need someone to cover a shift for an officer on hockey night? Ward volunteered himself. He even counted the time his officers spent at the games as duty hours. In other words, he was using public money to pay for the program's amenities as well as for the people who manned it. Naturally, he was getting increasing heat from some quarters over using government money on such fripperies. The atmosphere became so charged that Ward reluctantly decided to shut down the program. "I was tired of being beaten up about it," he told me.

The paperwork to end the Onside Program was on his desk when Ward's turn came to take students from his own adopted school to the game. One of the kids asked if he could bring a buddy, and Ward readily agreed, since he had an empty seat. The stranger turned out to be a boy whose father had recently died of cancer. "He was going through some really tough times," Ward recalled. "He was pretty messed up, and there were a lot of issues. I won't say that we solved them all that night, but we laughed and cried and talked, and I don't think we watched any of the game. We really connected."

It was during that talk, he told me, that Ward came to understand what courage really means for someone in a leadership position. "It's having the guts to stand up for your convictions in the face of adversity. Everyone is telling you that you are wrong, but you know that you are right. I knew I was right. We were right. It made sense."

He went back to the office and shredded the paperwork. Then he organized a campaign, starting with the schools, to win support for the program and convert the nonbelievers who saw it as nothing more than a giveaway to police officers. His renewed conviction led to the formation of a group of corporate sponsors who paid to spread the program to schools and police organizations all around the Calgary area, and even to expand it into the Canadian Football League with the Calgary Stampeders. "It was just a huge home run," Ward said. "Everybody wanted a piece of it."

Sometimes a leader has to have the courage of his convictions—and show it to the team, Ward told me. He still cherishes an old T-shirt printed with the logo of the Onside Program and the names of the corporate sponsors. "When I run into other tough things and I need a reminder of courage, I pull out that T-shirt," he said. "It's gotten pretty worn, but I wouldn't let my wife throw it out."

LESSON: Don't just accept change. Create it.

When Ward Clapham retires from the Royal Canadian Mounted Police, he plans to pass on the following key thoughts to his successors:

1. Change is inevitable.
2. Don't just accept it, own it.
3. Get out front and create change the way you want it; don't let somebody else call the shots.

When Ward started out in law enforcement, he told me, his "whole life revolved around how many crimes I could solve and how many people I could put in jail. That was the system I was working in. I decided that was going to change, that it made a lot more sense to prevent people from going into a life of crime while also putting away the people who were really evil."

Wherever he served in the years that followed, Ward worked actively to promote that change. He instilled in his people the importance of connecting on a personal level with the community in general, as well as with youngsters and adults who were at risk of becoming criminals. His focus was on finding ways to reach out to them, to win their trust, to go the extra mile to help them.

One of Ward's favorite stories is about a homeless man, a drug addict who lived under a bridge. At one point, the man tried to take his own life, but a police negotiator talked him out of it. A bond was created, and when the homeless man was feeling low, he would call the officer. As his life improved, the man continued to stay in touch, sharing news both good and bad with the officer. Eventually, the once-homeless drug addict became the chief executive officer of a major Canadian corporation. Still, he continued to call the officer to thank him, saying that "if you hadn't done what you did, I wouldn't be here today."

No, the officer wasn't Ward Clapham. But if Ward hadn't accomplished what he has in his astonishing career, that retrieved life wouldn't have happened.

COMMUNITY POLICING IS A COMMON TECHNIQUE IN Canada today, but Ward Clapham was there in the beginning—determining the shape it would take, leading the way, owning the change. It made a big difference for a lot of people whose lives might well have gone wrong otherwise. It also marked Ward as a dynamic, forward-looking leader, one with the courage of his convictions. When he saw change looming ahead, he didn't wait for it to push him around. He grabbed it by the horns and branded it as his own. That's what successful leaders do.

If you want your people to look constantly for new and better ways of doing their jobs, if you want them to head off problems before they damage your company, you have to set the example. Successful leaders stay ahead of the curve, seizing fresh ideas and burying stale ones, ever ready to adapt to change in a world that never stays put. That's how Ward Clapham inspires his Mounties, leading them to one breakthrough after another. You can do it too.

LESSONS

Play by the rules—usually.
Mutual respect is vital to team success.
Use informal leaders to help protect your flank.
Reach out to strengthen your team.
Challenge yourself, and grow.
Start small, and build from there.
Throw problems back to your people.
Help your team members grow.
Solve the real problem.
Look after your people first.
To lead your team, be part of it.
Stay focused on the real goal.
Show people that you care.
Never put down your people.
Stay close to your people.
When you know you're right, stick to your guns.
Don't just accept change. Create it.

EPILOGUE

AS THIS BOOK CLEARLY PROVES, THERE'S NO ONE-SIZE-FITS-all style of leadership. The remarkable men and women you met in these pages each have an overriding cause that spurs them on, and their individual techniques and lessons are tailored to that cause.

Al Collins works within the navy's system, and makes it work for him. Ward Clapham works constantly to change the Mounties' way of life. Trish Karter's overriding goal is to make the Dancing Deer Bakery a company that does good in the world. At BP, Laura Folse aims to get spiritual nourishment through her work, primarily by helping her people transcend their own shortcomings. Buddy Gengler saved his army platoon by having the guts to ask for help. Roger Valine proves that work and family can not only coexist in today's 24/7 world, but actually thrive.

But if there's no one formula, all of these unsung leaders nevertheless fit a general pattern of leadership. By no accident, it's the pattern I worked out for myself as the captain of USS *Benfold*.

My leaders begin with a feeling for people—the sense that everyone is worthwhile and has a contribution to make. My leaders instill mutual respect among all the people in their organizations, take pains to get to know their people, and genuinely care for all those they lead. They enlist people in the cause they are promoting. They try to help people grow and overcome hurdles. They encourage honest criticism and welcome new ideas from any source.

What my leaders get in return is wholehearted enthusiasm. Believing in the cause, the people they lead come to own it; the cause makes their work worth doing and gives their lives a larger meaning. As you have seen on page after page, this unswerving commitment provides an enormous boost for the people, the leader, and the enterprise alike. All of them have become true partners and collaborators, winners in any weather.

My leaders take risks, but never recklessly. They break rules, but always in the service of the cause. They fix problems, not blame; they prefer rewarding achievement to punishing failure. They encourage laughter, games, and a sense of fun as essential parts of the working environment, but all within the discipline of the overriding cause. And without exception, my leaders are simply nice people—men and women it is a pleasure to know.

There are other ways to lead, and they don't necessarily end in disaster. But if you follow the lessons in this book, you'll almost surely come out ahead. And though I don't guarantee success, I do make one solid promise: you'll have a good life. I've lived it, and I know.

INDEX

Antoniou, Ayis, 40, 42
Aquino, Corazon, 110

Badard, Darryl, 170
Barton, Darren, 118
Bethea, Dallas, 3
Browne, John, 144, 153
Bush, George H. W., 111
Bush, George W., xxvi

Cardinal, Perry, 174
Carney, Tom, 104
Clapham, Ward, xxvii, 156–96
Clinton, Bill, 75
Cochran, Patricia, 75, 76
Collins, Al, xxvi, 92–130, 196
Collins, Billie, 103, 104
Collins, Mary, 92, 93
Collins, Nemiah, 92
Custer, George, 97

Duffy, Mike, 80

Folse, Dan, 133
Folse, Laura, xxvi–xxvii, 131–55,
    196

Gengler, Gabriel J. "Buddy," III, xxv,
    1–38, 196
Gordon, Rachel, 61–62
Grubbs, Walter, 72, 73

Hallisey, Dave, 60
Harley, Jeff, 3–4, 7–9
Harris, Janice, 142
Hill, K. C., 59–60
Huber, Jerry, 124
Hugo, Victor, 74
Hurley, Frank, 166
Hussein, Saddam, 6, 97

Karter, Peter, 46
Karter, Trish, xxv, 39–67, 196
Kennedy, John F., Jr., 7

Lee, Robert E., 97
Lombardi, Suzanne, xxv, 40, 42, 61

Martinez, Drew, 13
McBurney, Lissa, 50–51, 53–54, 58,
    63–66
Moede, Scott, xxiii, 119
Moore, Edward, 124

Napoleon, 129
Nisco, Derek, 119–20

O'Donnell, John, 71
Orvis, Jim, 103–4, 105–7

Pearson, John, 121, 122
Perkins, Shaun, 148–49
Perry, William, 121
Pike, David, 142

Qaddafi, Muammar, 111

Rafalko, John, 142

Sandziuk, Peter, 178–79
Scheeler, Bob, 29–30
Schwarzenegger, Arnold, 1

Shackleton, Ernest, Sir, 165–67
Singer, Andy, 106
Slattery, Pat, 24–25
Smith, Ron, 174
Stuart, Jeb, 97

Valine, Anne, 71
Valine, Joe, 69–70
Valine, Lorraine, 69–70
Valine, Marie, 71, 75
Valine, Roger, xxvi, 68–91, 196

Wade, John, 60
Waters, Betty, 131
Waters, Spencer, 131
Webster, Hugh, 55

Yilmaz, Attila, 44